A STUDY OF

ARTHUR RIMBAUD

BY

HENRY MILLER

THE TIME OF THE ASSASSINS

THE TIME OF THE ASSASSINS

A Study of Rimbaud

BY HENRY MILLER

A New Directions Book

NEW DIRECTIONS BOOKS ARE PUBLISHED BY
JAMES LAUGHLIN AT NORFOLK, CONNECTICUT
NEW YORK OFFICE—333 SIXTH AVENUE

PREFACE

It was just a hundred years ago last October that Rimbaud was born. In France the centenary was celebrated in spectacular fashion. Celebrated writers the world over were invited to make the pilgrimage to Charleville, his birthplace. The festivities were in the nature of a national event. As for Rimbaud, he probably turned over in his grave.

Since his death portions of Rimbaud's voluminous work have been translated into many languages, among them Turkish and Bengali. Wherever there is still feeling for poetry and high adventure his name is a byword. In recent years the cult of Rimbaldiens has grown to amazing proportions and the literature devoted to his life and work increases by leaps and bounds. No other poet of modern times can be said to receive the same attention or consideration.

Aside from *A Season in Hell* and the *Illuminations*, only a small number of his poems have found their way into our language. Even these few translations reveal a wide and inevitable variety of interpretation. Yet however difficult and unseizable his style and thought may be, Rimbaud is not untranslatable. To do his work justice is another matter. In English we have yet to produce a poet who is able to do for Rimbaud what Baudelaire did for Poe's verse, or Nerval for *Faust,* or Morel and Larbaud for *Ulysses.*

I should like to make it clear that this little study, written ten years ago, is the outcome of a failure to translate, in the fashion intended, *A Season in Hell.* I still nourish the hope of rendering this text in a language more proximate to Rimbaud's own "nigger" tongue. The authors of *Really the Blues,* or a man like Lord Buckley,* are closer to Rimbaud, though they may not be aware of it, than the poets who have worshipped and imitated him.

What Rimbaud did for language, and not merely for poetry, is only beginning to be understood. And this more by readers than by writers, I feel. At least, in our country. Nearly all the modern French poets have been influenced by him. Indeed, one might say that contemporary French poetry owes everything to Rimbaud. Thus far, however, none have gone beyond him

* Get the album called "Euphoria," Vaya Records.

—in daring or invention. The only living poet who is able to give me anything approaching the pleasure and excitement of Rimbaud is St. John Perse. (His *Vents*, curiously enough, was translated by Hugh Chisholm here at Big Sur.)

The text herein reprinted originally appeared in two parts in the New Directions annual volumes, Nos. 9 and 11. Since then it has come out in French and in German, both editions published in Switzerland,* a country one is least apt to associate with Rimbaud's genius. In this publication the order of the two sections has been reversed. I ought perhaps to add that I had originally intended to write two more parts; I have since abandoned that idea.

It is my sincere belief that America needs to become acquainted with this legendary figure now more than ever. (The same is true of another extraordinary French poet who committed suicide a hundred years ago last January; Gérard de Nerval.) Never was there a time when the existence of the poet was more menaced than today. The American species, indeed, is in danger of being extinguished altogether.

When Kenneth Rexroth heard of the untimely death of Dylan Thomas he dashed off a "Me-

---

* The French edition published by Mermod, Lausanne, the German by Verlag der Arche, Zurich.

morial" called *Thou Shalt Not Kill*.* Written at white heat, and not intended for publication, it was nevertheless promptly circulated and translated into a number of languages. If one has any doubts about the fate which our society reserves for the poet, let him read this "Memorial" to the Welsh poet who wrote *Portrait of the Artist as a Young Dog.*

The status and condition of the poet—I use the word in the large as well as the strict sense—unquestionably reveal the true state of a people's vitality. China, Japan, India, Africa, *primitive* Africa, here poetry is still ineradicable. What we obviously lack in this country, what we are not even aware that we lack, is the dreamer, the inspired madman. With what ghoulish glee, when it comes time to shovel him under, do we focus attention upon the "maladaptation" of the lone individual, the only true rebel in a rotten society! Yet it is these very figures who give significance to that abused term "maladaptation."

In an article on "Baudelaire politique" in *Beaux-Arts*, January 25, 1955, Maurice Nadeau writes thus: "Dans *Mon Coeur Mis à Nu* il veut 'faire sentir sans cesse (qu'il se sent) étranger au

---

* Published by Horace Schwartz, P. O. Box 503, Sunnyvale, California, 1955.

monde et à ses cultes.' C'est le monde de la bourgeoisie dont 'la morale de comptoir' lui 'fait horreur,' 'un monde goulu, affamé de matérialités,' infatué de lui-même et qui ne s'aperçoit pas qu'il est entré en décadence, un monde que dans une singulière prophétie il voit de plus en plus 'américanisé,' 'voué a l'animalité,' 'où tout ce qui ne sera pas l'ardeur vers Plutus sera reputé un immense ridicule.' "

The impressive thing about the leading poets of the nineteenth century, and the twentieth as well, is their prophetic strain. Unlike Blake and Whitman, whose work is saturated with the ecstasy of a cosmic vision, our latter day poets dwell in the depths of a black forest. The spell of the millennium which obsessed such visionaries as Joachim of Floris, Hieronymus Bosch, Pico della Mirandola, and which today is tantalizingly more imminent than ever before, has been replaced by the thrall of utter annihilation. In the whirlpool of coming darkness and chaos—a veritable tohu-bohu—the poets of today are withdrawing, embalming themselves in a cryptic language which grows ever more and more unintelligible. And as they black out one by one, the countries which gave them birth plunge resolutely toward their doom.

The work of assassination, for such it is, will

soon reach its end. As the voice of the poet becomes stifled, history loses its meaning and the eschatological promise bursts like a new and frightening dawn upon the consciousness of man. Only now, at the edge of the precipice, is it possible to realize that "everything we are taught is false." The proof of this devastating utterance is demonstrable every day in every realm: on the battlefield, in the laboratory, in the factory, in the press, in the school, in the church. We live entirely in the past, nourished by dead thoughts, dead creeds, dead sciences. And it is the past which is engulfing us, not the future. The future always has and always will belong to—the poet.

Perhaps in fleeing from the world, Rimbaud preserved his soul from a fate worse than that which was allotted to him in Abyssinia. Perhaps *La Chasse Spirituelle*, if it is ever unearthed, will provide a clue now missing. Perhaps—who knows?—it will give us the link betwen *A Season in Hell* and that "Christmas on earth" which was once a reality to the adolescent dreamer.

In the symbolic language of the soul Rimbaud described all that is now happening. In my opinion, there is no discrepancy between his vision of the world, and of life eternal, and that of the great religious innovators. Over and over again we have been exhorted to create a new vision of heaven and earth, to begin afresh, to let the dead bury the dead, to live as brothers in the flesh, to make Christmas on earth a reality. And repeatedly we have been warned that unless the desire for a new life becomes a living conviction for each and every one of us, earthly existence can never be more than a Purgatory or a Hell. The one and only question which faces us is—how long can we postpone the inevitable?

When we reflect that it was a mere boy who shook the world by the ears, what are we to say? Is there not something just as *miraculous* about Rimbaud's appearance on this earth as there was in the awakening of Gautama, or in Christ's acceptance of the Cross, or in Joan of Arc's incredible mission of deliverance? Interpret his work as you like, explain his life as you will, still there is no living him down. The future is all his, even though there be no future.

HENRY MILLER
Big Sur, California

1955

PART I

Analogies, Affinities, Correspondences and
Repercussions

It was in 1927, in the sunken basement of a dingy house in Brooklyn, that I first heard Rimbaud's name mentioned. I was then 36 years old and in the depths of my own protracted Season in Hell. An absorbing book about Rimbaud was lying about the house but I never once glanced at it. The reason was that I loathed the woman who owned it and who was then living with us. In looks, temperament and behavior she was, as I later discovered, as near to resembling Rimbaud as it is possible to imagine.

As I say, though Rimbaud was the all engrossing topic of conversation between Thelma and my wife, I made no effort to know him. In fact, I fought like the very devil to put him out of my mind; it seemed to me then that he was the evil genius who had unwittingly inspired all my trouble and misery. I saw that Thelma, whom I despised, had identified herself with him, was imitating him as best she could, not only in her behavior but in the kind of verse she wrote. Everything conspired to make me repudiate his name, his influence, his very existence. I was then at the very lowest point of my whole career, my morale was completely shattered. I remember sitting in the cold dank basement trying to write by the light of a flickering candle with a pencil. I was trying to write a play depicting my own tragedy. I never succeeded in getting beyond the first act.

In that state of despair and sterility I was naturally highly sceptical of the genius of a seventeen-year-old poet. All that I heard about him sounded like an invention of crazy Thelma's. I was then capable of believing that she could conjure up subtle torments with which to plague me, since she hated me as much as I did her. The life which the three of us were leading, and which I tell about at length in *The Rosy Cruci-*

fixion, was like an episode in one of Dostoievsky's tales. It seems unreal and incredible to me now.

The point is, however, that Rimbaud's name stuck. Though I was not even to glance at his work until six or seven years later, at the home of Anais Nin in Louveciennes, his presence was always with me. It was a disturbing presence, too. "Some day you will have to come to grips with me." That's what his voice kept repeating in my ears. The day I read the first line of Rimbaud I suddenly remembered that it was of *Le Bateau Ivre* that Thelma had raved so much. *The Drunken Boat!* How expressive that title now seems in the light of all I subsequently experienced! Thelma meanwhile died in an insane asylum. And if I had not gone to Paris, begun to work there in earnest, I think my fate would have been the same. In that basement on Brooklyn Heights my own ship had foundered. When finally the keel burst asunder and I drifted out to the open sea, I realized that I was free, that the death I had gone through had liberated me.

If that period in Brooklyn represented my Season in Hell, then the Paris period, especially from 1932 to 1934, was the period of my Illuminations.

Coming upon Rimbaud's work at this time, when I had never been so fecund, so jubilant, so exalted, I had to push him aside, my own creations were more important to me. A mere glance at his writings and I knew what lay in store for me. He was pure dynamite, but I had first to fling my own stick. At this time I did not know anything about his life, except from the snatches Thelma had let drop years ago. I had yet to read a line of biography. It was in 1943, while living at Beverly Glen with John Dudley, the painter, that I first read about Rimbaud. I read Jean-Marie Carré's *A Season in Hell* and then Enid Starkie's work. I was overwhelmed, tongue-tied. It seemed to me that I had never read of a more accursed existence than Rimbaud's. I forgot completely about my own sufferings, which far outweighed his. I forgot about the frustrations and humiliations I had endured, the depths of despair and impotence to which I had sunk time and again. Like Thelma in the old days, I too could talk of nothing but Rimbaud. Everybody who came to the house had to listen to the song of Rimbaud.

It is only now, eighteen years after I first heard the name, that I am able to see him clearly, to read him like a clairvoyant. Now I *know* how great was his contribution, how terrible his tribulations. Now I understand the significance of his life and work—as much, that is, as one can say he understands the life and work of another. But what I see most clearly is how I miraculously escaped suffering the same vile fate.

Rimbaud experienced his great crisis when he was eighteen, at which moment in his life he had reached the edge of madness; from this point on his life is an unending desert. I reached mine at the age of thirty-six to thirty-seven, which is the age at which Rimbaud dies. From this point on my life begins to blossom. Rimbaud turned from literature to life; I did the reverse. Rimbaud fled from the chimeras he had created; I embraced them. Sobered by the folly and waste of mere experience of life, I halted and converted my energies to creation. I plunged into writing with the same fervor and zest that I had plunged into life. Instead of losing life, I gained life; miracle after miracle occurred, every misfortune being transformed to good account. Rimbaud, though plunging into a realm of incredible climates and landscapes, into a world of phantasy as strange and marvelous as his poems, became more and more bitter, taciturn, empty and sorrowful.

Rimbaud restored literature to life; I have endeavored to restore life to literature. In both of us the confessional quality is strong, the moral and spiritual preoccupation uppermost. The

flair for *language,* for music rather than literature, is another trait in common. With him I
have felt an underlying primitive nature which
manifests itself in strange ways. Claudel styled
Rimbaud "a mystic in the wild state." Nothing
could describe him better. He did not "belong"
—not anywhere. I have always had the same
feeling about myself. The parallels are endless.
I shall go into them in some detail, because in
reading the biographies and the letters I saw
these correspondences so clearly that I could not
resist making note of them. I do not think I am
unique in this respect; I think there are many
Rimbauds in this world and that their number
will increase with time. I think the Rimbaud
type will displace, in the world to come, the
Hamlet type and the Faustian type. The trend
is toward a deeper split. Until the old world dies
out utterly, the "abnormal" individual will tend
more and more to become the norm. The new
man will find himself only when the warfare
between the collectivity and the individual
ceases. Then we shall see the *human* type in its
fullness and splendor.

To get the full import of Rimbaud's Season in
Hell, which lasted eighteen years, one has to read

his letters. Most of this time was spent on the Somali Coast, in Aden a number of years. Here is a description of this hell on earth, from a letter to his mother:

"You cannot imagine the place: not a tree, even a withered one, not a sod of earth. Aden is the crater of an extinct volcano filled up with the sand of the sea. You only see lava and sand everywhere which cannot produce the slightest vegetation. It is surrounded by desert sands. Here the sides of the crater of our extinct volcano prevent the air from coming in and we are roasted as if in a lime-kiln."

How did a man of genius, a man of great energies, great resources, manage to coop himself up, to roast and squirm, in such a miserable hole? Here was a man for whom a thousand lives were not sufficient to explore the wonders of the earth, a man who broke with friends and relatives at an early age in order to experience life in its fullness, yet year after year we find him marooned in this hell-hole. How do you explain it? We know, of course, that he was straining at the leash all the time, that he was revolving countless schemes and projects to liberate himself, and liberate himself not only from Aden but from the whole world of sweat and struggle. Adventurer that he was, Rimbaud was nevertheless obsessed with the idea of attaining freedom, which he translated into terms of financial security. At the age of twenty-eight he writes home that the most important, the most urgent, thing for him is to become independent, no matter where. What he omitted to add was, *and no matter how*. He is a curious mixture of audacity and timidity. He has the courage to venture where no other white man has ever set foot, but he has not the courage to face life without a permanent income. He does not fear cannibals, but he fears his own white brethren. Though he is trying to amass a comfortable fortune, with which he can travel the globe leisurely and comfortably, or settle down somewhere should he find the right spot, he is still the poet and dreamer, the man who is unadapted to life, the man who believes in miracles, the man who is looking for Paradise in one form or another. At first he thinks that fifty thousand francs will be sufficient to secure him for life, but when he almost succeeds in accumulating this sum he decides that a hundred thousand would be safer. Those forty thousand francs! What a miserable, horrible time he has, carrying this nest egg about with him! It is practically his undoing. When they carry him down from Harar to the coast in a litter—a journey, incidentally, comparable to the Calvary—his thoughts are frequently on the gold in his belt. Even at the hospital in Marseilles, where his leg is amputated, he is plagued with this nest egg. If it is not the pain which keeps him awake nights it is the thought of the money which he has on him, which he has to hide so that it will not be stolen from him. He would like to put it in a bank, but how is he to get to a bank when he can't walk? He writes home begging some one to come and take care of his precious treasure. There is something so tragic and so farcical about this that one does not know what to say or think any more.

But what was at the root of this mania for security? The fear which every creative artist knows: that he is unwanted, that he is of no use in the world. How often in his letters does Rimbaud speak of being unfit to return to France and resume the life of the ordinary citizen. I have no trade, no profession, no friends there, he says. As do all poets, he sees the civilized world as the jungle; he does not know how to protect himself in it. Sometimes he adds that it is too late to think of returning—he is always speaking as though he were an old man!—he is too used to the free, wild, adventurous life to ever go back into harness again. The thing he had always loathed was honest toil, but in Africa,

9

Cyprus, Arabia, he toils like a nigger, depriving himself of everything, even coffee and tobacco, wearing a cotton shift year in and year out, putting aside every sou he makes, in the hope of one day buying his freedom. Even had he succeeded, we know he would never have felt free, never have been happy, never have thrown off the yoke of boredom. From the recklessness of youth he swerved to the cautiousness of old age. He was so utterly the outcast, the rebel, the accursed one, that nothing could save him.

I stress this aspect of his nature because it explains many of the malodorous traits attributed to him. He was not a miser, not a peasant at heart, as some of his biographers imply. He was not hard on others, he was hard with himself. Actually he had a generous nature. "His charity was lavish, unobtrusive and discreet," says his old employer, Bardey. "It is probably one of the few things he did without disgust and without a sneer of contempt."

There was one other bogey which obsessed him all his days and nights: military service. From the time he begins his wandering up until the day of his death he is tormented by the fear that he is not *en régle* with the military authorities. Just a few months before his death, while in the hospital at Marseilles, his leg amputated, his sufferings multiplying daily, the fear that the authorities will discover his whereabouts and send him to prison rest like an incubus upon him. *"La prison après ce que je viens de souffrir? Il vaudrait mieux la mort!"* He begs his sister to write him only when it is absolutely necessary, to address him not as Arthur Rimbaud but simply Rimbaud, and to post the letters from some neighboring town.

The whole fabric of his character is laid bare in these letters which are practically devoid of any literary quality or charm. We see his tremendous hunger for experience, his insatiable curiosity, his illimitable desires, his courage and tenacity, his self-flagellation, his asceticism, his sobriety, his fears and obsessions, his morbidity, his loneliness, his feeling of ostracism, and his unfathomable boredom. We see above all, that like most creative individuals, he was incapable of learning from experience. There is nothing but a repetitious round of similar trials and torments. We see him victimized by the illusion that freedom can be obtained by external means. We see him remaining the adolescent all his life, refusing to accept suffering or give it meaning. To estimate how great was the failure of the latter half of his life we have only to compare his journeying with that of Cabeza de Vaca.*

* See *The Power Within Us* by Haniel Long; Duell, Sloan & Pearce, New York.

But let us leave him in the midst of that desert which he created for himself. My purpose is to indicate certain affinities, analogies, correspondences and repercussions. Let us begin with the parents. Like Madame Rimbaud, my mother was the Northern type, cold, critical, proud, unforgiving, and puritanical. My father was of the South, of Bavarian parents, while Rimbaud's father was Burgundian. There was a continual strife and clash between mother and father, with the usual repercussions upon the offspring. The rebellious nature, so difficult to overcome, here finds its matrix. Like Rimbaud, I too began at an early age to cry: "Death to God!" It was death to everything which the parents endorsed or approved of. It extended even to their friends whom I openly insulted in their presence, even as a stripling. The antagonism never ceased until my father was virtually at the point of death, when at last I began to see how much I resembled him.

Like Rimbaud, I hated the place I was born in. I will hate it till my dying day. My earliest impulse is to break loose from the home, from the city I detest, from the country and its citizens with whom I feel nothing in common. Like him too, I am precocious, reciting verses in a foreign language while still in my high-chair. I learned to walk much ahead of time and to speak ahead of time, to read the newspaper even before I went to kindergarten. I was always the youngest in the class and not only the best student but the favorite of teachers and comrades alike. But, like him again, I despised the prizes and awards which were made me, and was expelled from school several times for refractory behavior. My whole mission, while at school, seemed to be to make fun of the teachers and the curriculum. It was all too easy and too stupid for me. I felt like a trained monkey.

From earliest childhood I was a voracious reader. For Christmas I requested only books, twenty and thirty at a time. Until I was twenty-five or so, I almost never left the house without one or more books under my arm. I read standing up, while going to work, often memorizing long passages of poetry from my favorite authors. One of these was Goethe's *Faust*, I remember. The chief result of this continuous absorption in books was to inflame me to further revolt, to stimulate the latent desire for travel and adventure, to make me anti-literary. It made me contemptuous of everything that surrounded me, alienating me gradually from my friends and imposing on me that solitary, eccentric nature which causes one to be styled a "bizarre" individual. From the age of eighteen (the year of Rimbaud's crisis) I became definitely unhappy, wretched, miserable, despondent. Nothing less than a complete change of environment seemed capable of dissipating this unchanging mood. At twenty-one I broke away, but not for long. Again, like Rimbaud, the opening flights were always disastrous. I was always returning home, either voluntarily or involuntarily, and always in a state of desperation. There seemed no egress, no way of achieving liberation. I undertook the most senseless labors, everything, in short, which I was unfitted for. Like Rimbaud in the quarries at Cyprus, I began with pick and shovel, a day laborer, a migratory worker, a vagabond. There was even this similarity, that when I broke from home it was with the intention of leading an outdoor life, of never again reading a book, of making a living with my two hands, of being a man of the open spaces and not a citizen of a town or city.

All the while, however, my language and my ideas betrayed me. I was completely the literary man, whether I wanted to be or not. Though I could get along with most any type of individual, especially the common man, in the end I was always suspect. It was very much like my visits to the library; always demanding the wrong book. No matter how large the library, the book I wanted was never in or else it was forbidden me. It seemed in those days that everything I wanted in life, or of life, was proscribed. Naturally, I was guilty of the most violent recriminations. My language, which had been shocking even as a child—I remember being dragged to the police station at the age of six for using foul language—my language, I say, became even more shocking and indecent.

What a jolt I got when I read that Rimbaud, as a young man, used to sign his letters—"that heartless wretch, Rimbaud." Heartless was an adjective I was fond of hearing applied to myself. I had no principles, no loyalty, no code whatsoever; when it suited me, I could be thoroughly unscrupulous, with friend and foe alike. I usually repaid kindness with insult and injury. I was insolent, arrogant, intolerant, violently prejudiced, relentlessly obstinate. In short, I had a distinctly disagreeable personality, a most difficult one to deal with. Yet I was very much liked; people seemed over-eager to forgive my bad qualities for the charm and enthusiasm I dispensed. This attitude served only to embolden me to take further liberties. Sometimes I myself wondered how on earth I could get away with it. The people I most loved to insult and injure were those who deemed themselves my superior in one way or another. Toward these I waged a relentless war. Beneath it all I was what you would call a good boy. My natural temperament was that of a kind, joyous, open-hearted individual. As a youngster I was often referred to as "an angel." But the demon of revolt had taken possession of me at a very early age. It was my mother who implanted it in me. It was against her, against all that she represented, that I directed my uncontrollable energy. Never until I was fifty did I once think of her with affection. Though she never actually balked me (only because my will was the stronger), I felt her shadow across my path constantly. It was a shadow of disapproval, silent and insidious, like a poison slowly injected into the veins.

I was amazed when I read that Rimbaud had allowed his mother to read the manuscript of *A Season in Hell*. Never did I dream of showing my parents anything I had written, or even discussing the subject of my writing with them. When I first informed them that I had decided to become a writer they were horrified; it was as though I had announced that I was going to become a criminal. Why couldn't I do something sensible, something that would enable me to gain a living? Never did they read a line of what

I have written. It was a sort of standing joke when their friends inquired of me, when they asked what I was doing. "*What is he doing?* Oh, he's writing. . . ." As though to say, he's crazy, he's making mud pies all day long.

I have always pictured the boy Rimbaud as being dolled up like a sissy, and later when a young man, as a dandy. That at any rate, was my case. My father being a tailor, it was natural for my parents to concentrate on my attire. When I grew up I inherited my father's rather elegant and sumptuous wardrobe. We were exactly the same size. But, like Rimbaud again, during the period when my individuality was asserting itself strenuously, I got myself up grotesquely, matching the inner eccentricities with the outer. I too was an object of ridicule in my own neighborhood. About this time I remember feeling extremely awkward, unsure of myself, and especially timid in conversation with men of any culture. "I don't know how to talk!" exclaimed Rimbaud in Paris when surrounded by other men of letters. Yet who could talk better than he when unrestrained? Even in Africa it was remarked of him how enchantingly he spoke at times. How well I understand this dilemma! What painful memories I have of stammering and stuttering in the presence of the men with whom I longed to hold conversation! With a nobody, on the other hand, I could talk with the tongues of angels. From childhood I was in love with the sound of words, with their magic, their power of enchantment. Often I went on verbal jags, so to speak. I could invent by the hour, driving my listeners to the point of hysteria. It was this quality, incidentally, which I recognized in Rimbaud the instant I glanced at a page of his. It registered like a shot. In Beverly Glen, when I was steeped in his life, I chalked up his phrases on the wall—in the kitchen, in the living room, in the toilet, even outside the house. Those phrases will never lose their potency for me. Each time I run across them I get the same thrill, the same jubilation, the same fear of losing my mind should I dwell on them too long. How many writers are there who can do this to you? Every writer produces some haunting passages, some memorable phrases, but with Rimbaud they are countless, they are strewn all over the pages, like gems tumbled from a rifled chest. It is this endowment which makes the link with Rimbaud indissoluble. And it is only this which I envy him for. Today, after all I have written, my deepest desire is to be done with the books I have projected and give myself up to the creation of sheer nonsense, sheer fantasy. I shall never be the poet he is, but there are vast imaginative reaches still to be attained.

And now we come to "the girl with the violet eyes." We know almost nothing about her. We know only that it was his first tragic experience of love. I do not know if it was in connection with her or the manufacturer's daughter that he used the words—"as scared as 36,000,000 new-born poodle dogs." But I can well believe that such must have been his reaction to the object of his affection. In any case I know that it was mine, and that she too had violet eyes. It is probable also, that like Rimbaud, I will think of her again on my dying bed. Everything is colored by that first disastrous experience. The strangest thing about it, I must add, is that it was not she who rejected me . . . it was I that held her in such awe and reverence that I fled from her. I imagine it must have been much the same in Rimbaud's case. With him, of course, everything —up to the eighteenth year—was packed into an incredibly short space of time. Just as he ran through the whole gamut of literature in a few years, so he ran through the course of ordinary experience quickly and briefly. He had but to taste a thing to know all that it promised or contained. And so his love life, so far as woman is concerned, was of cursory duration. We hear no mention of love again until Abyssinia, when he takes a native woman as a mistress. It is hardly love, one feels. If anything, his love was directed towards his Harari boy, Djami, to whom he tried to leave a legacy. It is hardly probable, knowing the life he led, that Rimbaud could have loved again with a whole heart.

Verlaine is reputed to have said of Rimbaud that he never gave himself, either to God or to man. How true this may be each one has to judge for himself. To me it seems that nobody could have desired to give himself more than Rimbaud did. As a boy he gave himself to God, as a young man he gave himself to the world. In both instances he felt that he had been deceived and betrayed; he recoiled, especially after his experience of the bloody Commune, and thereafter the core of his being remains intact, unyielding, inaccessible. In this respect he reminds me much of D. H. Lawrence, who had quite a little to say about this subject, i. e., about preserving intact the core of one's being.

It was from the moment he began to earn a living that his real difficulties set in. All his talents, and he possessed many, seemed of no use. Despite all reversals, he pushes on. "Advance, advance always!" His energy is boundless, his will indomitable, his hunger insatiable. "Let the poet burst with his straining after unheard of and unnameable things!" When I think of this period, marked by an almost frantic effort to make an entry into the world, to gain a toe-hold, when I think of the repeated sallies in this direction and that, like a beleaguered army trying to burst out of the grip in which it is held like a vise, I see my youthful self all over again. Thrice in his teens he reaches Brussels and Paris; twice he reaches London. From Stuttgart, after he has mastered sufficient German, he wanders on foot across Würtemberg and Switzerland into Italy. From Milan he sets out on foot for the Cyclades, via Brindisi, only to suffer a sunstroke and be returned to Marseilles via Leghorn. He covers the Scandinavian peninsula and Denmark with a traveling carnival; he ships from Hamburg, Antwerp, Rotterdam; he gets to Java by joining the Dutch army, only to desert after a taste of it. Passing St. Helena once in an English vessel which refuses to stop there, he jumps overboard but is brought back before he can reach the island. From Vienna he is escorted to the Bavarian border by the police, as a vagabond; from there he is brought under another escort to the Lorraine border. In all these flights and sallies he is always without money, always walking, and walking usually on an empty stomach. At

Civita Vecchia he is set ashore with gastric fever brought on by inflammation of the walls of the stomach caused by the friction of his ribs against his abdomen. Excessive walking. In Abyssinia it is excessive horseback riding. Everything to excess. He drives himself inhumanly. The goal is always beyond.

How well I understand his mania! Looking back upon my life in America, it seems to me that I covered thousands and thousands of miles on an empty stomach. Always looking for a few pennies, for a crust of bread, for a job, for a place to flop. Always looking for a friendly face! At times, even though I was hungry, I would take to the road, hail a passing car and let the driver deposit me where he liked, just to get a change of scene. I know thousands of restaurants in New York, not from visiting them as a patron but from standing outside and gazing wistfully at the diners seated at the tables inside. I can still recall the odor of certain stands on street corners where hot dogs were being served. I can still see the white-robed chefs in the windows flipping waffles or flapjacks into the pan. Sometimes I think I was born hungry. And with the hunger is associated the walking, the tramping, the searching, the feverish, aimless to and fro. If I succeeded in begging a little more than was necessary for a meal I went immediately to the theatre or to a movie. All I cared for, once my stomach was filled, was to find a warm, cozy place where I could relax and forget my troubles for an hour or two. I would never save enough for carfare in those circumstances; leaving the womblike warmth of the theatre, I would set out in cold or rain to walk to the remote place where I happened to live. From the heart of Brooklyn to the heart of Manhattan I have walked countless times, in all kinds of weather and in varying degrees of starvation. When utterly exhausted, when unable to move another step, I have been obliged to turn round and retrace my steps. I understand perfectly how men can be trained to make forced marches of phenomenal length on empty bellies.

But it is one thing to walk the streets of your native city amidst hostile faces and quite another to tramp the highway in neighboring states. In your home town the hostility is merely indifference; in a strange town, or in the open stretches between towns, it is a distinctly antagonistic element that greets you. There are savage dogs, shot guns, sheriffs and vigilantes of all sorts lying in wait for you. You dare not lie down on the cold earth if you are a stranger in that vicinity. You keep moving, moving, moving all the time. In your back you feel the cold muzzle of a revolver, bidding you to move faster, faster, faster. This is your own country, too, in which all this happens, not a foreign land. The Japs may be cruel, the Huns barbarous, but what devils are these who look like you and talk like you, who wear the same dress, eat the same food, and who hound you like dogs? Are these not the worst enemies a man can have? The others I can find excuses for, but for one's own kind I can find no excuse whatever. "I have no friends there," Rimbaud often wrote home. Even in June, 1891, from the hospital in Marseilles, he repeats this refrain. *"Je mourrai où me jettera le destin. J'espère pouvoir retourner là où j'étais (Abysinnie), j'y ai des amis de dix ans, qui auront pitié de moi, je trouverai chez eux du travail, je vivrai comme je pourrai. Je vivrai toujours là-bas, tandis qu'en France, hors vous, je n'ai ni amis, ni connaissances, ni personne."* Here a footnote reads: *"Cependant la gloire littérarire de Rimbaud battait alors son plein à Paris. Les admirateurs, qui lui eussent été personellement tout devoués, étaient d'éjà nombreux. Il l'ignorait. Quelle malédiction!"*

Yes, what a malediction! I think of my own return to New York, an enforced return also, after ten years abroad. I had left America with

24

ten dollars which I borrowed at the last moment before catching the boat; I returned without a cent, borrowing the money for the cabman from the hotel clerk who, seeing my trunk and valises, assumed I would have the money to pay for my hotel bill. The first thing I have to do, on arriving "home," is to telephone some one for a little money. Unlike Rimbaud, I have no belt full of gold hidden under the bed; but I still have two good legs, and in the morning, if help does not arrive during the night, I shall begin walking uptown in search of a friendly face again. In those ten years abroad I too had worked like a demon; I had earned the right to live comfortably for a year or so. But the war intervened, smashed everything, just as the intrigues of the European powers had blighted Rimbaud's chances in Somaliland. How familiar sounds a passage from a letter dated Aden, January 1888 . . . *"Tous les gouvernements sont venus engloutir des millions (et même en somme quelques milliards) sur toutes ces côtes maudites, désolées, où les indigènes errent des mois sans vivre et sans eau, sous le climat le plus effroyable du globe; et tous ces millions qu'on a jetés dans le ventre des bédouins n'ont rien rapporté que les guerres, les désastres de tous genres!"*

What a faithful picture this is of our dear governments! Always seeking to gain a foothold in some ungodly place, always suppressing or exterminating the natives, always clinging to their ill-gotten gains, defending their possessions, their colonies, with army and navy. For the biggest ones the world is not big enough. For the little ones who need room, pious words and veiled threats. The earth belongs to the strong, to those with the biggest armies and navies, to those who wield the economic big stick. How ironical that the solitary poet who ran to the end of the world in order to eke out a miserable living should have to sit with hands folded and watch the big powers make a mess of things in his own garden.

"Yes, the end of the world . . . Advance, advance always! Now begins the great adventure . . ." But as fast as you advance, the government is there ahead of you, with restrictions, with shackles and manacles, with poison gases, tanks and stink bombs. Rimbaud the poet sets himself to teaching the Harari boys and girls the Koran in their own language. The governments would sell them in slavery. "There is some destruction that is necessary," he wrote once, and what a fuss has been made over that simple statement! He was speaking then of the destruction incidental to creation. But governments destroy without the slightest excuse, and certainly with never a thought of creation. What Rimbaud the poet desired was to see the old forms go, in life as well as in literature. What governments desire is to preserve the status quo, no matter how much slaughter and destruction it entails. Some of his biographers, in describing his behavior as a youth, make him out to be a very bad boy; he did such nasty things, don't you know. But when it comes to appraising the activities of their dear governments, particularly with regard to those shady intrigues which Rimbaud inveighed against, they are all honey and white-wash. When they want to castigate him as the adventurer, they speak of what a great poet he was; when they want to subjugate him as a poet they speak of his chaos and rebelliousness. They are aghast when the poet imitates their plunderers and exploiters, and they are horrified when he shows no concern for money or for the monotonous, irksome life of the ordinary citizen. As a Bohemian he is too Bohemian, as a poet too poetical, as a pioneer too pioneering, as a man of affairs too much the man of affairs, as a gunrunner too clever a gunrunner, and so on and so forth. Whatever he did, he did too well, that seems to be the complaint against him. The pity is that he didn't become a politician. He would have done the job so well that Hitler, Stalin and

Mussolini, to say nothing of Churchill and Roosevelt, would seem like mountebanks today. I don't think he would have brought about quite the destruction which these estimable leaders visited upon the world. He would have kept something up his sleeve for a rainy day, so to speak. He would not have shot his bolt. He would not have lost track of the goal, as our brilliant leaders seem to have done. No matter what a fiasco he made of his own life, oddly enough I believe that if he had been given the chance he would have made the world a better place to live in. I believe that the dreamer, no matter how impractical he may appear to the man in the street, is a thousand times more capable, more efficient, than the so-called statesman. All those incredible projects which Rimbaud envisaged putting into effect, and which were frustrated for one reason or another, have since been realized in some degree. He thought of them too soon, that was all. He saw far beyond the hopes and dreams of ordinary men and statesmen alike. He lacked the support of those very people who delight in accusing him of being the dreamer, the people who dream only when they fall asleep, never with eyes wide-open. For the dreamer who stands in the very midst of reality all proceeds too slowly, too lumberingly—even destruction.

"He will never be satisfied," writes one biographer. "Under his weary glance all flowers fade, all stars pale." Yes, there is a grain of truth in this. I know because I suffer from the same disease. *But,* if one has dreamed an empire, the empire of man, and if one dares to reflect at what a snail's pace men are advancing toward the realization of this dream, it is quite possible that what are called the activities of man pale to insignificance. I don't believe for a minute that the flowers ever faded or the stars were ever dimmed in Rimbaud's eyes. I think that with these the core of his being always maintained a direct and fervid communication. It was in the world of men that his weary glance saw things pale and fade. He began by wanting to "see all, feel all, exhaust everything, explore everything, say everything." It was not long before he felt the bit in his mouth, the spurs in his flanks, the lash on his back. Let a man but dress differently from his fellow creatures and he becomes an object of scorn and ridicule. The only law which is really lived up to whole-heartedly and with a vengeance is the law of conformity. No wonder that as a mere lad he ended "by finding the disorder of his mind sacred." At this point he had really made himself a seer. He found, however, that he was regarded as a clown and a mountebank. He had the choice of fighting for the rest of his life to hold the ground he had gained or to renounce the struggle utterly. Why could he not have compromised? Because compromise was not in his vocabulary. He was a fanatic from childhood, a person who had to go the whole hog or die. In this lies his purity, his innocence.

In all this I rediscover my own plight. I have never relinquished the struggle. But what a price I have paid! I have had to wage guerilla warfare, that hopeless struggle which is born only of desperation. The work I set out to write has not yet been written, or only partially. Just to raise my voice, to speak in my own fashion, I have had to fight every inch of the way. The song has almost been forgotten for the fight. Talk of the weary glance under which flowers fade and stars pale! My glance has become positively corrosive: it is only a miracle that under my pitiless gaze they are not blasted away. So much for the core of my being. As for the superficies, well, the outward man has gradually learned to accommodate himself to the ways of the world. He can be in it without being of it. He can be kind, gentle, charitable, hospitable. Why not? "The real problem," as Rimbaud pointed out, "is to make the soul monstrous." That is to say, not hideous but prodigious! What is the meaning of monstrous? According to the dictionary, "any organized form of life greatly malformed either by the lack, excess, misplacement or distortion of parts or organs; hence, anything hideous or abnormal, or made up of inconsistent parts or characters, whether repulsive or not." The root is from the Latin verb *moneo,* to warn. In mythology we recognize the monstrous under the form of the harpy, the gorgon, the sphinx, the centaur, the dryad, the mermaid. They are all prodigies, which is the essential meaning of the word. They have upset the norm, the balance. What does this signify if not the fear of the little man. Timid souls always see monsters in their path, whether these be called hippogriffs or Hitlerians. Man's greatest dread is the expansion of consciousness. All the fearsome, gruesome part of mythology stems from this fear. "Let us live in peace and harmony!" begs the little man. But the law of the universe dictates that peace and harmony can only be won by inner struggle. The little man does not want to pay the price for that kind of peace and harmony; he wants it ready-made, like a suit of manufactured clothes.

There are obsessive, repetitive words which a writer uses which are more revealing than all the facts which are amassed by patient biographers. Here are a few that we come across in Rimbaud's work: *éternité, infini, charité, solitude, angoisse, lumiére, aube, soleil, amour, beauté, inoui, pitié, démon, ange, ivresse, paradis, enfer, ennui.* . . .

These are the warp and woof of his inner pattern; they tell us of his innocence, his hunger, his restlessness, his fanaticism, his intolerance, his absolutism. His god was Baudelaire who had plumbed the depths of evil. I have remarked before, and it is worth repeating, that the whole nineteenth century was tormented with the question of God. Outwardly it seems like a century given up to material progress, a century of discoveries and inventions, all pertaining to the physical world. At the core, however, where the artists and thinkers are always anchored, we observe a profound disturbance. Rimbaud epitomizes the conflict in a few pages. And, as if that were not enough, he impresses on his whole life the same enigmatic cast which characterizes the epoch. He is more truly the man of his time than were Goethe, Shelley, Blake, Nietzsche, Hegel, Marx, Dostoievsky. He is split from top to toe in every realm of his being. He faces two ways always. He is torn apart, racked by the wheel of time. He is the victim and the executioner: when you speak his name you have the time, the place and the event. Now that we have succeeded in breaking down the atom the cosmos is split wide open. Now we face in every direction at once. We have arrived, possessed of a power which even the gods of old could not wield. We are there, before the gates of hell. Will we storm the gates, burst hell itself wide open? I believe we will. I think that the task of the future is to explore the domain of evil until not a shred of mystery is left. We shall discover the bitter roots of beauty, accept root and flower, leaf and bud. We can no longer resist evil: we must accept.

When he was writing his "nigger book" (*Une Saison en Enfer*), Rimbaud is said to have declared: "My fate depends on this book!" How profoundly true that statement was not even Rimbaud himself knew. As we begin to realize our own tragic fate, we begin to perceive what he meant. He had identified his fate with that of the most crucial epoch known to man. Either, like him, we are going to renounce all that our civilization has stood for thus far, and attempt to build afresh, or we are going to destroy it with our own hands. When the poet stands at nadir the world must indeed be upside down. If the poet can no longer speak for society, but only for himself, then we are at the last ditch.

33

On the poetic corpse of Rimbaud we have begun erecting a tower of Babel. It means nothing that we still have poets, or that some of them are still intelligible, still able to communicate with the mob. What is the trend of poetry and where is the link between poet and audience? *What is the message?* Let us ask that above all. Whose voice is it that now makes itself heard, the poet's or the scientist's? Are we thinking of Beauty, however bitter, or are we thinking of atomic energy? And what is the chief emotion which our great discoveries now inspire? Dread! We have knowledge without wisdom, comfort without security, belief without faith. The poetry of life is expressed only in terms of the mathematical, the physical, the chemical. The poet is a pariah, an anomaly. He is on the way to extinction. Who cares now how *monstrous* he makes himself? The monster is at large, roaming the world. He has escaped from the laboratory; he is at the service of any one who has the courage to employ him. The world has indeed become number. The moral dichotomy, like all dichotomies, has broken down. This is the period of flux and hazard; the great drift has set in.

And fools are talking about reparations, inquisitions, retribution, about alignments and coalitions, about free trade and economic stabilization and rehabilitation. No one believes in his heart that the world situation can be righted. Everyone is waiting for the great event, the only event which preoccupies us night and day: *the next war*. We have unsettled everything; no one knows how or where to reach for the control. The brakes are still there, but will they work? We know they won't. No, the demon has broken loose. The age of electricity is as far behind us as the Stone Age. This is the Age of Power, power pure and simple. Now it is either heaven or hell, no in between is possible any longer. And by all indications we will choose hell. When the poet lives his hell, it is no longer possible for the common man to escape it. Did I call Rimbaud a renegade? *We are all renegades*. We have been reneging since the dawn of time. Fate at last is catching up with us. We are going to have our Season in Hell, every man, woman and child identified with this civilization. This is what we have been begging for, and now it is here. Aden will seem like a comfortable place. In Rimbaud's time it was still possible to leave Aden for Harar, but fifty years from now the earth itself will be one vast crater. Despite the denials of the men of science, the power we now have in our hands *is* radioactive, *is* permanently destructive. We have never thought of power in terms of good,

35

only in terms of evil. There is nothing mysterious about the energies of the atom; the mystery is in men's hearts. The discovery of atomic energy is synchronous with the discovery that we can never trust one another again. There lies the fatality—in this hydra-headed fear which no bomb can destroy. The real renegade is the man who has lost faith in his fellowman. Today the loss of faith is universal. Here God himself is powerless. We have put our faith in the bomb, and it is the bomb which will answer our prayers.

What a shock it is for the poet to discover that Rimbaud renounced his calling! It is like saying that he renounced Love. Whatever the motive, certainly the paramount drive was loss of faith. The consternation of the poet, his feeling of betrayal and deception, is paralleled by the reaction of the scientist when he discovers the use to which his inventions are put. One is tempted to compare Rimbaud's act of renunciation with the release of the atomic bomb. The repercussions, though more wide-spread in the latter case, are not more profound. The heart registers a shock before the rest of the body. It takes time for doom to spread throughout the corpus of civilization. But when Rimbaud walked out the back door, doom had already announced itself.

How right I was to put off the true discovery of Rimbaud! If I draw entirely different conclusions from other poets about his appearance and manifestations on earth, it is in the same spirit that the saints drew extraordinary conclusions about the coming of Christ. Either such things are signal events in the history of man or the art of interpretation is a bogus one. That we shall all live one day as did Christ I have not the slightest doubt. That we shall all deny our individuality first, I have no doubt about either. We have reached the ultimate point of egotism, the atomic state of being. There we go to smash. We are preparing now for the death of the little self in order that the real self may emerge. Unwittingly and unconsciously we have made the world one, but one in nullity. We must go through a collective death in order to emerge as genuine individuals. If it is true, as Lautréamont said, that "poetry must be made by all," then we must find a new language in which one heart will speak to another without intermediation. Our appeal to one another must be as direct and instantaneous as is the man of God's to God. The poet today is obliged to surrender his calling because he has already evinced his despair, because he has already acknowledged his inability to communicate. To be a poet was once the highest calling; today it is the most futile one. It is so not because the world is immune to the poet's pleading, but because the poet himself no longer believes in his divine mission. He has been singing off-key now for a century or more; at last we can no longer tune in. The screech of the bomb still makes sense to us, but the ravings of the poet seem like gibberish. And it *is* gibberish if, out of two billion people who make up the world, only a few thousand pretend to understand what the individual poet is saying. The cult of art reaches its end when it exists only for a precious handful of men and women. Then it is no longer art but the cipher language of a secret society for the propagation of meaningless individuality. Art is something which stirs men's passions, which gives vision, lucidity, courage and faith. Has any artist in words of recent years stirred the world as did Hitler? Has any poem shocked the world as did the atomic bomb recently? Not since the coming of Christ have we seen such vistas unfolding, multiplying daily. What weapons has the poet compared to these? *Or what dreams?* Where now is his vaunted imagination? Reality is here before our very eyes, stark naked, but where is the song to announce it? Is there a poet of even the fifth magnitude visible? I see none. I do not call poets those who make verses, rhymed or unrhymed. I call that man poet who is capable of profoundly altering the world. If there be such a poet living in our midst, let him declare himself. Let him raise his voice! But it will have to be a voice which can drown the roar of the bomb. He will have to use a language which melts men's hearts, which makes the blood bubble.

If the mission of poetry is to awaken, we ought to have been awakened long ago. Some have been awakened, there is no denying that. But now *all* men have to be awakened—and immediately—or we perish. But man will never perish, depend on that. It is a culture, a civilization, a way of life which will perish. When these dead awaken, as they will, poetry will be the very stuff of life. We can afford to lose the poet if we are to preserve poetry itself. It does not require paper and ink to create poetry or to disseminate it. Primitive peoples on the whole are poets of action, poets of life. They are still making poetry, though it moves us not. Were we alive to the poetic, we would not be immune to their way of life: we would have incorporated their poetry in ours, we would have infused our lives with the beauty which permeates theirs. The poetry of the civilized man has always been exclusive, esoteric. It has brought about its own demise.

"We must be absolutely modern," said Rimbaud, meaning that chimeras are out of date, and superstitions and fetiches and creeds and dogmas and all the cherished drivel and inanity of which our vaunted civilization is composed. We must bring light, not artificial illumination. "Money is depreciating everywhere," he wrote in one of his letters. That was back in the '80's. Today in Europe it has practically no value whatever. What men want is food, shelter, clothing—basic things—not money. The rotten edifice has crumbled before our very eyes, but we are reluctant to believe our eyes. We still hope to be able to do business as usual. We neither realize the damage that has been done nor the possibilities of rebirth. We are using the language of the Old Stone Age. If men cannot grasp the enormity of the present how will they ever be able to think in terms of the future? We have been thinking in terms of the past for several thousand years. Now, at one stroke, that whole mysterious past has been obliterated. There is only the future staring us in the face. It yawns like a gulf. It is terrifying, everyone concedes, even to begin to think what the future holds in store for us. Far more terrifying than the past ever was. In the past the monsters were of human proportions; one could cope with them, if one were heroic enough. Now the monster is invisible; there are billions of them in a grain of dust. I am still using the language of the Old Stone Age, you will notice. I speak as though the atom itself were the monster, as though *it* exercised the power and not us. This is the sort of deception we have practised on ourselves ever since man began to think. And this, too, is a delusion—to pretend that at some distant point in the past man *began to think*. Man has not even begun to think. Mentally, he is still on all fours. He is groping about in the mist, his eyes closed, his heart hammering with fear. And what he fears most—God pity him!—is his own image.

If a single atom contains so much energy, what about man himself in whom there are universes of atoms? If it is energy he worships, why does he not look at himself? If he can conceive, and demonstrate to his own satisfaction, the boundless energy imprisoned in an infinitesimal atom, what then of those Niagaras within him? And what of the earth's energy, to speak of but another infinitesimal conglomeration of matter? If we are looking for demons to harness, then there is such an infinitude of them that the thought is paralyzing. *Or*—it is so exalting that men should be running breathlessly from door to door spreading delirium and pandemonium.

Only now perhaps can one possibly appreciate the fervor which was Satan's when he unleashed the forces of evil. Historical man has known nothing of the truly demonic. He has inhabited a shadow world filled with faint reverberations only. The issue between good and evil was decided long ago. Evil belongs to the phantom world, the world of make-believe. Death to the chimeras! Aye, but they *were* slain long ago. Man was given second sight that he might see through and beyond the world of phantasmagoria. The only effort demanded of him is that he open the eyes of his soul, that he gaze into the heart of reality and not flounder about in the realm of illusion and delusion.

There is one subtle change I feel compelled to make, in connection with the interpretation of Rimbaud's life, and this concerns the element of fate. It was his destiny to be the electrifying poet of our age, the symbol of the disruptive forces which are now making themselves manifest. It was his *fate,* I used to think, to be ensnared into a life of action in which he would end ingloriously. When he said that his fate depended on the *"Saison,"* he meant, I assume, that it would decide the course of his future actions, and, as now seems clear, it most certainly did. We may think, if we like, that in writing it he stood so clearly revealed to himself that he no longer had need for expression on the level of art. As poet he had said all he possibly could say. We imagine that he was aware of this and consequently turned his back on art deliberately. Some men have referred to the second half of his life as a sort of Rip Van Winkle sleep; it is not the first time that an artist has gone to sleep on the world. Paul Valéry, who leaps to mind immediately, did something of the sort when he deserted the realm of poetry for mathematics for a period of twenty years or so. Usually there has been a return, or an awakening. In Rimbaud's case the awakening was in death. The little light which flickered out with his demise grew in power and intensity as the fact of his death became more largely known. He has lived more wondrously and vividly since he departed this earth than he ever did in life. One wonders, had he come back *in this life,* what sort of poetry he would have written, what his message would have been. It was as though, cut off in the prime of manhood, he was cheated of that final phase of development which permits a man to harmonize his warring selves. Operating under a curse for the major part of his life, fighting with all his powers to find egress into the clear, open spaces of his being, he is beaten to earth for the last time just when one feels that the clouds were lifting. The feverishness of his activity bespeaks the consciousness of a short life, as in the case of D. H. Lawrence and others. If one asks whether such men realized themselves to the fullest one is inclined to reply in the affirmative. Yet they were not permitted to run full cycle; if we are to be fair to them, this unlived future must be taken into consideration. I have said it of Lawrence, and I will say it of Rimbaud, that had they been granted another thirty years of life, they would have sung a different tune entirely. They were at one with their destiny always; it was their fate which betrayed them and which is apt to deceive us in examining their deeds and motives.

Rimbaud, as I see him, was *par excellence* an evolving type. The evolution he went through in the first half of his life is no more amazing than the evolution of the second half. It is we, perhaps, who are unaware of the glorious phase he was preparing to enter. He sinks below our horizon on the eve of another great change, at the beginning of a fruitful period when the poet and the man of action were about to fuse. We see him expiring as a defeated man; we have no perception of the rewards which his years of worldly experience were storing up for him. We see two opposite types of being united in one man; we see the conflict but not the potential harmony or resolution. Only those who are interested in the *significance* of his life will permit themselves to dally with such speculations. Yet the only purpose in going to the life of a great personality, of studying it in conjunction with his work, is to bring forth what is hidden and obscure, what was uncompleted, as it were. To speak of the real Lawrence or the real Rimbaud is to make cognizant the fact that there is an *unknown* Lawrence, an *unknown* Rimbaud. There would be no controversy about such figures had they been able to reveal themselves utterly. It is curious to note in this connection that it is precisely the men who deal in revelations—*self-revelations*—about whom there is the greatest mystery. Such individuals seem to be born into the world struggling to express what is most secret in their nature. That there is a secret which gnaws them is hardly a matter of doubt. One need not be "occult" to be aware of the difference between their problems and other eminent men's, as well as their approach to these problems. These men are deeply allied to the spirit of the times, to those underlying problems which beset the age and give it its character and tone. They are always dual, apparently, and for a good reason, since they incarnate the old and the new together. It is for this reason that more time, more detachment, is required to appreciate and evaluate them than their contemporaries however illustrious. These men have their roots in that very future which disturbs us so profoundly. They have two rhythms, two faces, two interpretations. They are integrated to transition, to flux. Wise in a new way, their language seems cryptic to us, if not foolish or contradictory.

In one of the poems Rimbaud makes mention of that gnawing secret I refer to:

> *"Hydre intime, sans gueules,*
> *Qui mine et désole."*

It was an affliction which poisoned him both at the zenith and the nadir of his being. In him sun and moon were both strong, and both eclipsed. (*"Toute lune est atroce et tout soleil amer."*) The very core of his being was corroded; it spread, like the cancer which attacked his knee. His life as a poet, which was the lunar phase of his evolution, reveals the same quality of eclipse as his later life of adventurer and man of action, which was the solar phase. Narrowly escaping madness in his youth, he escaped it once again upon his death. The only solution possible for him, had he not been cut off by death, was the contemplative life, the mystic way. It is my belief that his thirty-seven years were a preparation for such a way of life.

Why do I permit myself to speak of this unfinished part of his life with such certitude? Because once again I see analogies to my own life, my own development. Had I died at the age Rimbaud died, what would be known of my purpose, my efforts? Nothing. I would have been regarded as a rank failure. I had to wait until my forty-third year to see my first book published. It is a fateful event for me, comparable in every way to the publication of the *"Saison."* With its advent a long cycle of frustration and defeat comes to an end. For me it might also be styled "my nigger book." It is the last word in despair, revolt and malediction. It is also prophetic and healing, not only for my readers but for me too. It has that saving quality of art which so often distinguishes those books which break with the past. It enabled me to close the door on the past and re-enter it by the back door. The gnawing secret continues to eat me away, but now it is "the open secret," and I can cope with it.

And what is the nature of this secret? I can only say that it has to do with the mothers. I feel that it was the same with Lawrence and with Rimbaud. All the rebelliousness which I share with them derives from this problem which, as nearly as I can express it, means the search for one's true link with humanity. One finds it neither in the personal life nor in the collective life, if one is of this type. One is unadaptable to the point of madness. One longs to find his peer, but one is surrounded by vast empty spaces. One needs a teacher, but one lacks the humility, the flexibility, the patience which is demanded. One is not even at home or at ease with the great in spirit; even the highest are defective or suspect. And yet one has affinities only with these highest types. It is a dilemma of the first magnitude, a dilemma fraught with the highest significance. One has to establish the ultimate difference of his own peculiar being and doing so discover his kinship with all humanity, even the very lowest. Acceptance is the key word. But acceptance is precisely the great stumbling block. It has to be total acceptance and not conformity.

What makes it so difficult for this type to accept the world? The fact, as I see it now, that in early life the whole dark side of life, and of one's own being, of course, had been suppressed, so thoroughly repressed as to be unrecognizable. Not to have rejected this dark side of being would have meant, so one unconsciously reasons with himself, a loss of individuality, loss of freedom even more. Freedom is bound up with differentiation. Salvation here means only the preservation of one's unique identity in a world tending to make every one and every thing alike. This is the root of the fear. Rimbaud stressed the fact that he wanted *liberty* in salvation. But one is saved only by surrendering this illusory freedom. The liberty he demanded was freedom for his ego to assert itself unrestrained. That is not freedom. Under this illusion one can, if one lives long enough, play out every facet of one's being and still find cause to complain, ground to rebel. It is a kind of liberty which grants one the right to object, to secede if necessary. It does not take into account other people's differences, only one's own. It will never aid one to find one's link, one's communion, with all mankind. One remains forever separate, forever isolate.

All this has but one meaning for me—that one is still bound to the mother. All one's rebellion was but dust in the eye, the frantic attempt to conceal this bondage. Men of this stamp are always against their native land—impossible to

49

be otherwise. Enslavement is the great bugaboo, whether it be to country, church or society. Their lives are spent in breaking fetters, but the secret bondage gnaws at their vitals and gives them no rest. They must come to terms with the mother before they can rid themselves of the obsession of fetters. "Outside! Forever outside! Sitting on the doorstep of the mother's womb." I believe those are my own words, in *Black Spring*, a golden period when I was almost in possession of the secret. No wonder one is alienated from the mother. One does not notice her, except as an obstacle. One wants the comfort and security of her womb, that darkness and ease which for the unborn is the equivalent of illumination and acceptance for the truly born. Society is made up of closed doors, of taboos, laws, repressions and suppressions. One has no way of getting to grips with those elements which make up society and through which one must work if one is ever to establish a true society. It is a perpetual dance on the edge of the crater. One may be acclaimed as a great rebel, but one will never be loved. And for the rebel above all men it is necessary to know love, to give it even more than to receive it, and to be it even more than to give it.

Once I wrote an essay called "The Enormous

Womb." In this essay I conceived the world itself as a womb, as the place of creation. This was a valiant and a valid effort toward acceptance. It was a harbinger of a more genuine acceptance which was shortly to follow, an acceptance which I realized with my whole being. But this attitude, of regarding the world itself as womb and creation, was not a pleasant one to other rebels. It only alienated me still more. When the rebel falls out with the rebel, as he usually does, it is like the ground giving way beneath one's feet. Rimbaud experienced that sinking feeling during the Commune. The professional rebel finds it difficult to swallow such an attitude. He has an ugly name for it: treason. But it is just this treasonable nature in the rebel which differentiates him from the herd. He is treasonable and sacrilegious always, if not in the letter then in the spirit. He is a traitor at heart because he fears the humanity in him which would unite him with his fellow man; he is an iconoclast because, revering the image too greatly, he comes to fear it. What he wants above all is his common humanity, his powers of adoration and reverence. He is sick of standing alone; he does not want to be forever a fish out of water. He cannot live with his ideals unless these ideals are shared, but how can he communicate his ideas and ideals if he does not speak the same language as his fellow man? How can he win them if he does not know love? How can he persuade them to build if his whole life is spent in destroying?

Upon what foundation is unrest built? The *"hydre intime"* eats away until even the core of one's being becomes sawdust and the whole body, one's own and the world's, is like unto a temple of desolation. *"Rien de rien ne m'illusionne!"* cried Rimbaud. Yet his whole life was nothing but a grand illusion. The true reality of his being he never uncovered, never came to grips with. Reality was the mask which he struggled with fierce claws to rip away. In him was a thirst unquenchable.

> *"Légendes ni figures*
> *Ne me désaltèrent."*

No, nothing could quench his thirst. The fever was in his vitals where the secret gnawed and gnawed. His spirit reveals itself from the amniotic depths, where, like a drunken boat, he tosses on the sea of his poems. Wherever the light penetrates it wounds. Each message from the bright world of spirit creates a fissure in the wall of the tomb. He lives in an ancestral refuge which crumbles with exposure to the light of day. With all that was elemental he was at home;

he was a throwback, an archaic figure, more French than any Frenchman yet an alien in their midst. Everything that had been reared in the light of common effort he rejected. His memory, which embraces the time of the Cathedrals, the time of the Crusades, is a race memory. It is almost as though birth had failed to individualize him. He comes into the world equipped like a Saracen. He has another code, another principle of action, another world view. He is a primitive endowed with all the noblesse of ancient lineage. He is super in every way, the better to conceal his minus side. He is that differentiated being, the prodigy, born of human flesh and blood but suckled by the wolves. No analytic jargon will ever explain the monster. We know what he failed to do, but what he should have done, in order to be true to his being, who can say? We have to revise the laws of understanding in order to grapple with such an enigma.

Men are being thrown up now who will force us to alter our methods of perception. That ancient refuge in which Rimbaud lived with his secret is fast crumbling. Every discordant figure will soon be forced into the open; there are no hiding places left any more. In the common plight the bizarre figure with his mysterious malady will be routed from his unique trench. The entire world of men and women is being rounded up, brought before the bars of justice. What matter if some rare spirits were ill at ease, maladjusted, distilling perfume from their sufferings? Now the race as a whole is preparing to suffer the great ordeal. With the great event almost upon us the reading of the glyphs becomes more than ever important, more than ever exciting. Soon, and most abruptly, we shall all be swimming breast to breast, the seer as well as the common man. A world totally new, a world awesome and forbidding, is at our door. We shall awaken one day to look out upon a scene beyond all comprehending. The poets and seers have been announcing that new world for generations, but we have refused to believe them. We of the fixed stars have rejected the message of the wanderers in the sky. We have regarded them as dead planets, as fugitive ghosts, as the survivors of long forgotten catastrophes.

How like the wanderers of the heavens are the poets! Do they not, like the planets, seem to be in communication with other worlds? Do they not tell us of things to come as well as of things long past, buried in the racial memory of man? What better significance can we give to their fugitive stay on earth than that of emissaries from another world? We live amidst dead fact whereas they live in signs and symbols. Their longings coincide with ours only when we approach perihelion. They are trying to detach us from our moorings; they urge us to fly with them on the wings of the spirit. They are always announcing the advent of things to come and we crucify them because we live in dread of the unknown. In the poet the springs of action are hidden. A more highly evolved type than the rest of the species—and here by "poet" I mean all those who dwell in the spirit and the imagination—he is allowed only the same period of gestation as other men. He has to continue his gestation after birth. The world he will inhabit is not the same as ours; it resembles ours only insofar as our world may be said to resemble that of the Cro-Magnon man. His apprehension of things is similar to that of a man from a fourth-dimensional world living in one of three dimensions. He is in our world but not of it; his allegiance is elsewhere. It is his mission to seduce us, to render intolerable this limited world which bounds us. But only those are capable of following the call who have lived through their three-dimensional world, have lived out its possibilities.

The signs and symbols which the poet employs are one of the surest proofs that language is a means of dealing with the unutterable and the inscrutable. As soon as the symbols become communicable on every level they lose their validity and effectiveness. To ask the poet to speak the language of the man in the street is like expecting the prophet to make clear his predictions. That which speaks to us from higher, more distant, realms comes clothed in secrecy and mystery. That which is being constantly expanded and elaborated through explication—in short, the conceptual world—is at the same time being compressed, tightened up, through the use of the stenographic calligraphy of symbols. We can never explain except in terms of new conundrums. What belongs to the realm of spirit, or the eternal, evades all explanation. The language of the poet is asymptotic; it runs parallel to the inner voice when the latter approaches the infinitude of spirit. It is through this inner register that the man without language, so to speak, is in communication with the poet. There is no question of verbal education involved but one of spiritual development. The purity of Rimbaud is nowhere more apparent than in this uncompromising pitch which he maintained throughout his work. He is understood by the most diverse types, as well as misunderstood by the most diverse types. His imitators can be detected immediately. He has nothing in common with the school of symbolists. Nor has he anything in common with the surrealists, as far as I can see. He is the father of many schools and the parent of none. It is his unique use of the symbol which is the warrant of his genius. This symbology was forged in blood and anguish. It was at once a protest and a circumvention of the dismal spread of knowledge which threatened to stifle the source of the spirit. It was also a window opening upon a world of vastly more complex relations for which the old sign language no longer served. Here he is closer to the mathematician and the scientist than to the poet of our time. Unlike our latter-day poets, be it noted, he did *not* make use of the symbols used by the mathematician and the scientists. His language is the language of the spirit, not of weights, measures and abstract relations. In this alone he revealed how absolutely "modern" he was.

Here I should like to amplify a point I touched on earlier, the matter of communication between poet and audience. In applauding Rimbaud's use of the symbol I mean to emphasize that in this direction lies the true trend of the poet. There is a vast difference, in my mind, between the use of a more symbolic script and the use of a more highly personal jargon which I referred to as "gibberish." The modern poet seems to turn his back on his audience, as if he held it in contempt. In self-defense he will sometimes liken himself to the mathematician or the physicist who has now come to employ a sign language wholly beyond the comprehension of most educated people, an esoteric language understandable only to the members of his own cult. He seems to forget that he has a totally different function than these men who deal with the physical or the abstract world. His medium is the spirit and his relation to the world of men and women is a vital one. His language is not for the laboratory but for the recesses of the heart. If he renounces the power to move us his medium becomes worthless. The place of renewal is the heart, and there the poet must anchor himself. The scientist, on the other hand, is utterly concerned with the world of illusion, the physical world in which things *are made to happen*. He is already a victim of the powers he once hoped to exploit. His day is coming to a close. The poet will never quite find himself in this position. He would not be a poet in the first place if his instinct for life were as perverted as the scientist's. But the danger which menaces him is the abrogation of his powers; by betraying his trust he is surrendering the destinies of countless human beings to the control of worldly individuals whose sole aim is their own personal aggrandizement. The abdication of Rimbaud is of another caliber from the self-liquidation of the contemporary poet. Rimbaud refused to become something other than he was, in his office as poet, in order to survive. Our poets are jealous of the name but show no disposition to accept the responsibility of their office. They have not *proved* themselves poets; they are content simply to call themselves such. They are writing not for a world which hangs on their every word but for one another. They justify their impotence by deliberately making themselves unintelligible. They are locked in their glorified little egos; they hold themselves aloof from the world for fear of being shattered at the first contact. They are not even personal, when one gets right down to it, for if they were we might understand their torment and delirium, such as it is. They have made themselves as abstract as the problems of the physicist. Theirs is a womblike yearning for a world of pure poetry in which the effort to communicate is reduced to zero.*

* See the essay called "An Open Letter to Surrealists Everywhere" in *The Cosmological Eye,* New Directions, New York.

When I think of those other great spirits who were contemporaneous with Rimbaud—men like Nietzsche, Strindberg, Dostoievsky—when I thing of the anguish they suffered, an ordeal beyond anything our men of genius have had to endure, I begin to think that the latter half of the nineteenth century was one of the most accursed periods in history. Of that band of martyrs, all of them filled with premonitions of the future, the one whose tragedy most closely approaches Rimbaud's is Van Gogh. Born a year ahead of Rimbaud he dies by his own hand at almost the same age. Like Rimbaud, he too had an adamant will, an almost superhuman courage, an extraordinary energy and perseverance, all of which enabled him to fight against insuperable odds. But as with Rimbaud, the struggle exhausts him in the prime of life; he is laid low at the height of his powers.

The wanderings, the changes of occupation, the vicissitudes, the frustrations and humiliations, the cloud of unknowingness which surrounded them, all these factors common to both their lives, make them stand out like ill-fated twins. Their lives are among the very saddest we have record of in modern times. No man can read Van Gogh's letters without breaking down time and again. The great difference between them, however, is in the fact that Van Gogh's life inspires. Shortly after Van Gogh's death Dr. Gachet, who understood his patient profoundly, wrote to Vincent's brother, Theo: "The word love of art is not exact, one must call it *faith*, a faith to which Vincent fell a martyr!" This is the element which seems to be entirely missing in Rimbaud—faith, whether in God, man or art. It is the absence of this which makes his life seem gray and at times pure black. Nevertheless, the similarities of temperament between the two men are most numerous and striking. The greatest bond between them is the purity of their art. The measure of this purity is given in terms of suffering. With the turn of the century this sort of anguish seems no longer possible. We enter a new climate, not a better one necessarily, but one in which the artist becomes more callous, more indifferent. Whoever now experiences anything approaching that sort of agony, and registers it, is branded as "an incurable romantic." One is not expected to *feel* that way any longer.

In July 1880, Van Gogh wrote to his brother one of those letters which goes to the heart of things, a letter that draws blood. In reading it one is reminded of Rimbaud. Often in their letters there is an identity of utterance which is striking. Never are they more united than when they are defending themselves against unjust accusations. In this particular letter Van Gogh is defending himself against the aspersion of idleness. He describes in detail two kinds of idleness, the evil sort and the profitable sort. It is a veritable sermon on the subject, and worth returning to again and again. In one part of this letter we hear the echo of Rimbaud's very words . . . "So you must not think that I disavow things," he writes. "I am rather faithful in my unfaithfulness, and though changed, I am the same, and my only anxiety is: how can I be of use in the world, cannot I serve some purpose and be of any good, how can I learn more and study profoundly certain subjects? You see, that is what preoccupies me constantly, and then I feel myself imprisoned by poverty, excluded from participating in certain work, and certain necessary things are beyond my reach. That is one reason for not being without melancholy, and then one feels an emptiness where there might be friendship and strong and serious affections, and one feels a terrible discouragement gnawing at one's very moral energy, and fate seems to put a barrier to the instincts of affection, and a flood of disgust rises to choke one. And one exclaims: 'How long, my God!' "

Then he goes on to differentiate between the man who is idle from laziness, from lack of character, from the baseness of his nature, and the other sort of idle man who is idle in spite of himself, who is inwardly consumed by a great longing for action, who does nothing because it is impossible for him to do anything, and so on. He draws a picture of the bird in the gilded cage. And then he adds—pathetic, heart-rending, fateful words—: "And men are often prevented by circumstances from doing things, a prisoner in I do not know what horrible, horrible, most horrible cage. There is also, I know it, the deliverance, the tardy deliverance. A just or unjustly ruined reputation, poverty, fatal circumstances, adversity, that is what it is that keeps us shut in, confines us, seems to bury us, but, however, one feels certain barriers, certain gates, certain walls. Is all this imagination, fantasy? I do not think so. And then one asks: 'My God! is it for long, is it for ever, is it for eternity?' Do you know what frees one from this captivity? It is every deep, serious affection. Being friends, being brothers, love, that is what opens the prison by supreme power, by some magic force. But without this one remains in prison. There where sympathy is renewed, life is restored."

What a parallel there is between Rimbaud's

exiled existence among the natives of Abyssinia and Van Gogh's voluntary retirement amidst the inmates of a lunatic asylum! Yet it was in these bizarre settings that both men found a relative measure of peace and satisfaction. For eight years, says Enid Starkie, "Rimbaud's sole friend and comforter seems to have been Djami, the Harari boy of fourteen or fifteen, his body servant, his constant companion . . . Djami was one of the few people in his life whom he remembered and talked of with affection, the only friend of whom he spoke on his deathbed, when the thoughts of other men usually turn to those whom they have known in their early youth." As for Van Gogh, it is the postman Roulin who stands by him in the darkest hours. His great longing to find some one with whom he could live and work never materialized in the outside world. The experience with Gauguin was not only disastrous but fatal. When at last he found the good Dr. Gachet at Auvers it was too late, his moral fiber had been sapped. "To suffer without complaint is the only lesson we have to learn in this life." That was the conclusion Van Gogh drew from his bitter experience. It is on this note of supreme resignation that his life comes to an end. Van Gogh passed away in July 1890. A year later Rimbaud writes to his relatives: *"Adieu mariage, adieu famille, adieu avenir! Ma vie est passée. Je ne suis plus qu'un tronçon immobile."*

No two men more ardently desired liberty and freedom than these two imprisoned spirits. Both seemed to deliberately choose the most difficult path for themselves. For both the cup of bitterness was filled to overflowing. In both men there lived a wound which never healed. Some eight years before his death, Van Gogh reveals in one of his letters what the second great disappointment in love had done to him. "A single word made me feel that nothing is changed in me about it, that it is and remains a wound, which I carry with me, but it lies deep and will never heal, it will remain in after years just what it was the first day." Something of the sort happened to Rimbaud, also; though we know almost nothing about this unhappy affair, it is hard not to believe that the effect was equally devastating.

There is one quality which they had in common which also deserves to be noticed—the utter simplicity of their daily requirements. They were ascetic as only saints can be. It is thought that Rimbaud lived poorly because he was miserly. But when he had amassed a considerable sum he showed himself willing to part with it at the first call. Writing to his mother from Harar in 1881, he says: "*Si vous avez besoin, prenez de quoi est à moi: c'est à vous. Pour moi, je n'ai personne à qui songer, sauf ma propre personne, qui ne demande rien.*" When one thinks that these men, whose work has been an unending source of inspiration to succeeding generations, were forced to live like slaves, that they had difficulty in securing their sustenance, which was hardly more than a coolie demands, what are we to think of the society from which they sprang? Is it not evident that such a society is preparing its own rapid downfall? In one of his letters from Harar, Rimbaud contrasts the natives of Abyssinia with the civilized whites. "*Les gens du Harar ne sont ni plus bêtes, ni plus canailles, que les nègres blancs des pays dit civilisés; ce n'est pas du même ordre, voilà tout. Ils sont même moins méchants, et peuvent, dans certain cas, manifester la reconnaissance et de la fidelité. Il s'agit d'être humain avec eux.*" Like Van Gogh, he was more at home with the despised and the downtrodden than with men of his own milieu. Rimbaud took a native woman to satisfy his affection, while Van Gogh acted as a husband (and father of her children) to an unfortunate woman inferior to him in every way, a woman who made his life unbearable. Even in the matter of carnal love they were denied the privileges of the ordinary man. The less they demanded of life the less they received. They lived like scarecrows, amidst the abundant riches of our cultural world. Yet no two men of their time could be said to have refined their senses in anticipation of a feast more than they. In the space of a few years they had not only eaten up, but eaten through, the accumulated heritage of several thousand years. They were faced with starvation in the midst of seeming plenty. It was high time to give up the ghost. Europe was already actively preparing to destroy the mould which had grown to fit like a coffin. The years which had intervened since their death belong to that dark side of life in whose shadow they had struggled to breathe. All that is barbarous, false, unlived out, is coming to the surface with the force of an eruption. We are beginning at last to realize how very unmodern is this boasted "modern" age. The truly modern spirits we have done our best to kill off. Their yearning does indeed seem romantic now; they spoke the language of the soul. We are now talking a dead language, each a different one. Communication is finished; we have only to deliver the corpse.

"I shall probably leave for Zanzibar next month," Rimbaud writes in one of his letters. In another he is thinking of going to China or to India. Every now and then he inquires what news about the canal (Panama)? He will travel to the end of the earth if there is hope there of eking out a living. It never occurs to him to return to his own country and begin life anew. It is always the exotic place to which his mind turns.

What a familiar chord that strikes! How often, in the early days, I dreamed of going to Timbuctoo! If that were impossible, then to Alaska or the Polynesian Islands. In the Trocadero Museum once I stood gazing for a long time at the faces of the natives in the Caroline Islands. As I studied their beautiful features I recalled that distant relatives of ours had settled there. If I could ever get there, I thought, I would feel "at home" at last. As for the Orient, that has always been in the back of my head, a longing which began early in childhood. Not only China and India, but Java, Bali, Burma, the state of Nepal, Tibet. Never once has it occurred to me that I would have difficulties in those faraway places. It always seemed to me that I would be welcomed with open arms. To return to New York, on the other hand, was a frightening thought. The city whose every street I know like a book, where I have so many friends, remains the last place on earth I would turn to.

I would rather die than be forced to spend the rest of my days in the place of my birth. I can only visualize myself returning to New York as utterly destitute, as a cripple, as a man who has given up the ghost.

With what curiosity I read the early letters of Rimbaud! He has just begun his wanderings; he rambles on discursively about the sights he has seen, the nature of the land, the trifles which the folks at home always read with delight and excitement. He is certain that when he gets to his destination he will find suitable employment. He is sure of himself, everything will go well. He is young, full of high spirits, and there is so much to see in this great world. It does not take long for the tone to change. For all the verve and ebullience he displays, for all his willingness to work, for all that he possesses in the way of talent, ingenuity, doggedness, adaptability, he discovers before very long that there is really no place for a person like himself anywhere. The world does not want originality; it wants conformity, slaves, more slaves. The place for the genius is in the gutter, digging ditches, or in the mines or quarries, somewhere where his talents will *not* be employed. A genius looking for employment is one of the saddest sights in the world. He fits in nowhere, nobody wants him.

He is maladapted, says the world. With that, the doors are rudely slammed in his face. But is there no place at all for him, then? Oh yes, there is always room at the very bottom. Have you never seen him along the waterfront loading sacks of coffee or some other "necessary" commodity? Have you not observed how well he washes dishes in the kitchen of a filthy restaurant? Have you not seen him lugging bags and valises at the railway station?

I was born in New York where there is every opportunity to succeed, as the world imagines. It is not so difficult for me to visualize myself standing in line at the employment agencies and the charity bureaus. The only job I ever seemed capable of filling in those days was that of dishwasher. And then I was always too late. There are thousands of men always ready and eager to wash dishes. Often I surrendered my place to another poor devil who seemed to me a thousand timse worse off than myself. Sometimes, on the other hand, I borrowed money for car fare or a meal from one of the applicants in line and then forgot all about getting a job. If I saw an ad for something I liked better in a neighboring city I would go there first, even if it meant wasting the whole day to get there. I've several times traveled a thousand miles and more in quest of a chimerical job, a job as waiter, for example. Often the thought of adventure stimulated me to go far-afield. I might pick up a conversation with a man en route which would alter the whole course of my life. I might "sell" myself to him, just because I was so desperate. So I reasoned to myself. Sometimes I was offered the job I went in search of, but knowing deep down that I could never hold it, I would turn round and go home again. Always on an empty stomach, to be sure. All arrivals and departures were on an empty stomach. That is the second thing always associated with genius—the lack of food. In the first place he is not wanted, in the second place there is no food for him. And in the third place he knows not where to lay his head. Aside from these discomforts he leads, as every one knows, the life of Reilly. He is lazy, shiftless, unstable, treacherous, a liar, a thief, a vagabond. He causes dissatisfaction wherever he roams. Truly, an impossible person. Who can get along with him? No one, not even himself.

Why harp on the ugly, the discordant things? The life of a genius is not all dirt and misery. Every one has his troubles, whether he is a genius or not. Yes, that is true too. And nobody appreciates that truth more than the man of genius. Every now and then you will find the genius coming forth with a plan to save the world, or a method of regeneration, at least. These are laughed off as wild dreams, as thoroughly Utopian. "Christmas on Earth!" for example. What a coke dream! Let him first prove that he can navigate on his own, you say. How can he save others if he is incapable of saving himself? The classic answer. Irrefutable. But the genius never learns. He was born with the dream of Paradise, and no matter how crazy it sounds, he will struggle to make it realizable again and again. He is incorrigible, a recidivist in every sense of the word. He understands the past, he embraces the future—but the present is meaningless to him. Success holds no bait for him. He spurns all rewards, all opportunities. He is a malcontent. Even when you accept his work, he has no use for you. He is already engaged on another work; his orientation has shifted, his enthusiasm is elsewhere. What can you do for him? How can you appease him? You can do nothing. He is beyond reach. He is after the impossible.

This unlovely image of the man of genius is, I think, a fairly accurate one. Though somewhat different, necessarily, it probably describes the plight of the unusual man even in primitive societies. The primitives too have their misfits, their neurotics, their psychopaths. We persist, nevertheless, in believing that this condition need not be so, that a day may come when this type of individual will not only find a place in the world but be honored and looked up to. Maybe this is a coke dream too. Maybe adaptation, harmony, peace and communion are varieties of mirage which will forever delude us. The fact, however, that we created these concepts, that they have the deepest meaning for us, means that they are realizable. They may have been created out of need, but they will become realities through desire. The man of genius usually lives *as if* these dreams were possible of fulfillment. He is too charged with the potency of them to live them out for himself; he is, in this sense, akin to those supreme renunciators who refuse Nirvana until all men are able to realize it with them.

"The golden birds which flit through the umbrage of his poems!" Whence came those golden birds of Rimbaud's? And whither do they fly? They are neither doves nor vultures; they inhabit the airs. They are private messengers hatched in darkness and released in the light of illumination. They bear no resemblance to the creatures of the air, neither are they angels. They are the rare birds of the spirit, birds of passage who flit from sun to sun. They are not

73

imprisoned in the poems, they are liberated there. They rise with wings of ecstasy and vanish in the flame.

Conditioned to ecstasy, the poet is like a gorgeous unknown bird mired in the ashes of thought. If he succeeds in freeing himself, it is to make a sacrificial flight to the sun. His dreams of a regenerate world are but the reverberations of his own fevered pulse beats. He imagines the world will follow him, but in the blue he finds himself alone. Alone but surrounded by his creations; sustained, therefore, to meet the supreme sacrifice. The impossible has been achieved; the duologue of author with Author is consummated. And now forever through the ages the song expands, warming all hearts, penetrating all minds. At the periphery the world is dying away; at the center it glows like a live coal. In the great solar heart of the universe the golden birds are gathered in unison. There it is forever dawn, forever peace, harmony and communion. Man does not look to the sun in vain; he demands light and warmth not for the corpse which he will one day discard but for his inner being. His greatest desire is to burn with ecstasy, to commerge his little flame with the central fire of the universe. If he accords the angels wings so that they may come to him with messages of peace, harmony and radiance from worlds beyond, it is only to nourish his own dreams of flight, to sustain his own belief that he will one day reach beyond himself, and on wings of gold.

One creation matches another; in essence they are all alike. The brotherhood of man consists not in thinking alike, nor in acting alike, but in aspiring to praise creation. The song of creation springs from the ruins of earthly endeavor. The outer man dies away in order to reveal the golden bird which is winging its way toward divinity.

PART II

When Do Angels Cease to Resemble Themselves?

There is a passage in *A Season in Hell* (the section called "The Impossible") which seems to provide the clue to the nature of the harrowing tragedy which Rimbaud's life describes. That this is his last work—at the age of eighteen! —has a certain importance. Here his life divides evenly in two, or to look at it another way, it completes itself. Like Lucifer, Rimbaud succeeds in getting himself ejected from Heaven, the Heaven of Youth. He is vanquished not by an Archangel but by his own mother, who for him personifies authority. It is a fate which he

77

abetted from the very beginning. The brilliant youth who possesses all talents, and who despises them, abruptly breaks his life in two. It is an act at once magnificent and horrible. Satan himself could not have devised a more cruel punishment than Arthur Rimbaud meted out to himself in his invincible pride and egotism. At the very threshold of manhood he surrenders his treasure (the genius of the creator) to "that secret instinct and power of death in us" which Amiel has described so well. The *"hydre intime"* so deforms the image of love that only defiance and impotence are discernible finally. Abandoning all hope of recovering the key to his lost innocence, Rimbaud plunges into the black pit in which the human spirit touches nadir, there to parody Krishna's words: "With this myself I establish the whole Universe, and remain for ever separate."

The passage which reveals his awareness of the issue and his choice, which is necessitous, runs as follows:

"If my spirit were always wide-awake from this moment on, we would soon arrive at the truth, which perhaps even now surrounds us with her angels, weeping! . . . If it had been awake up until now, I would not have given in to degenerate instincts, to a forgotten epoch!

. . . If it had always been wide-awake, I would be sailing in full wisdom! . . ."

What it was that sealed his vision, and thereby brought about his doom, no one knows—and probably no one ever will know. His life, for all the facts at our disposal, remains as much a mystery as his genius. What we see clearly enough is that everything he prophesied about himself in the three years of illumination vouchsafed him is fulfilled in the years of wandering when he makes of himself a desert. How often in his writings appear the words desert, ennui, rage, toil! In the second half of his life these words attain a concrete significance which is devastating. He becomes everything that he predicted, everything that he was frightened of, everything that he raged against. The struggle to free himself of man-made fetters, to rise above human laws, codes, conventions, superstitions leads him nowhere. He becomes the slave of his own whims and caprices, a puppet who has nothing better to do than chalk up a few more trifling crimes to his credit in the log book of his own damnation.

That he gives in at the end when his body is but "a motionless stump," as he puts it, is not to be dismissed with the sceptic's sneer. Rimbaud was the rebel incarnate. It required every known degradation and humiliation, every form of laceration, to break the stubborn will which had been perverted at the source. He was perverse, untractable, adamant—until the very last hour. Until there was no more hope. He was one of the most desperate souls that ever stalked the earth. True, he gave up from exhaustion—but not before he had traveled every wrong road. At the end, having nothing to sustain his pride any longer, having nothing to look forward to except the jaws of death, deserted by all but the sister who loved him, there is nothing to do but to scream for mercy. His soul has been vanquished, it can but surrender. Long ago he had written: "*Je est un autre.*" Now the problem of "making the soul monstrous in the manner of the comprachicoes" reaches solution. That other self which was the I abdicates. It had known a long, hard reign; it had withstood every siege only to fall apart finally and dissolve into nothingness.

"I say that you must be a Seer . . . make yourself a Seer!" he had urged at the beginning of his career. And then suddenly it is over, his career, and he has no use for literature, not even his own. Then the trek, the desert, the burden of guilt, boredom, rage, toil—and humiliation, loneliness, pain, frustration, defeat and surrender. Out of this wilderness of conflicting emotions, out of the battlefield which he has made of his own mortal body, there blossoms in the very last hour the flower of faith. How the angels must have rejoiced! Never was there a more recalcitrant spirit than this proud Prince Arthur! Let us not overlook the fact that the poet who boasted that he had inherited his idolatry and love of sacrilege from his ancestors, the Gauls, was known in school as "the dirty little bigot." It was a sobriquet which he acknowledged with pride. Always "with pride." Whether it was the hoodlum in him or the bigot, the deserter or the slave-dealer, the angel or the demon, it is always with pride that he records the fact. But in the end it is the priest who shrives him who may be said to walk off with pride. To Rimbaud's sister Isabelle he is reported to have said: "Your brother has faith, my child . . . He has faith, and I have never beheld such faith."

It is the faith of one of the most desperate souls that ever thirsted for life. It is the faith born of the last hour, the last minute—*but it is faith.* What does it matter, therefore, how long he resisted, or how defiantly and tempestuously? He was not poor in spirit, he was mighty. He fought with every last ounce of strength that was in him. And that is why his name, like Lucifer's, will ever remain a glorious one, why he will be claimed by this side and that. Even his enemies claim him! We know how the monument which was erected to him in his native town of Charleville was decapitated by the Germans and carried off during the last war's invasion. How memorable, how prophetic, now seem the words which he flung at his friend Delahaye when the latter referred to the indubitable superiority of the German conquerors. "The idiots! Behind their blaring trumpets and beating drums they will return to their own country to eat sausages, believing that it is all over. But wait a little. Now they are all militarized from top to toe, and for a long time they will swallow all the rubbish of glory under treacherous masters who will never let go of them . . . I can see from now the rule of iron and madness that will imprison all of German society. And all that merely to be crushed in the end by some coalition!"

Yes, he may be claimed with equal justice by both sides. That is his glory, I repeat. It means that he embraced the darkness *and* the light. What he walked out on was the world of living death, the false world of culture and civilization. He denuded his spirit of all the artificial trappings which sustain the modern man. *"Il faut être absolument moderne!"* The *"absolument"* is important. A few sentences later he adds: "The battle of the spirit is as brutal as the battle of men; but the vision of justice is the pleasure of God alone." The implication is that we are experiencing a false modernity: with us there is no sharp and brutal combat, no heroic struggle such as the saints of old waged. The saints were strong men, he maintains, and the hermits were artists, no longer in style now, alas! Only a man who knew the meaning of temptation could speak thus. Only a man who valued discipline, the discipline which seeks to raise life to the level of art, could thus extol the holy ones.

In a sense, Rimbaud's whole life may be said to be a search for the proper discipline, one, to be sure, which would give him freedom. In the beginning, as innovator, this is obvious enough, even though one may quarrel with the sort of discipline which he imposes upon himself. In the second half of his life, when he has broken with society, the purpose of his Spartan discipline is more obscure. Is it merely to become a worldly success that he endures all those hardships and privations? I doubt it. Superficially he may seem to have no greater goal or purpose than any ambitious adventurer. That is the view of cynics, of failures who would love to have as company such a great figure as the engimatic Rimbaud. To me it seems that he was preparing his own Calvary. Though he may not have understood it himself, his behavior comes close to resembling that of the saint struggling with his own savage nature. Blindly, perhaps, he seems to be making himself ready to receive the divine grace which he had rashly and ignorantly spurned in his youth. One may also say that he was digging his own grave. But it was never the grave he was interested in—he had a supreme horror of the worms. For him death had already made itself all too manifest in the French way of life. Remember his terrible words . . . "to lift with dry fist the lid of the coffin, to sit down, to suffocate. Thus, no old age at all, no dangers; terror is not French." It was fear of this living death which made him choose the hard life; he was willing to brave every terror rather than surrender in midstream. What then was the purpose, the goal, of such a strenuous life? For one thing, of course, it was to explore every possible phase of life. He thought of the world as "full of magnificent places that could not be visited within the lives of a thousand men." He demanded a world "in which his immense energy could work unhampered." He wanted to exhaust his powers in order to realize himself absolutely. In the ultimate, however, his ambition was to arrive, even if utterly beaten and exhausted, at the frontier of some dazzling new world, a world which would bear no resemblance to the one he knew.

What other world could this be than the shining world of the spirit? Does not the soul always express itself in terms of youth? From Abyssinia, Rimbaud once wrote in despair to his mother: "We live and die by another pattern than we could ever have designed, and that without hope of any kind of compensation. We are lucky that this is the only life we shall have to live, and that that is obvious . . ." He was not *always* so certain that this is the only life. Does he not wonder, during his season in Hell, if there may be other lives? He suspects there are. And that is part of his torment. Nobody, I venture to say, knew better than the young poet that for every failed or wasted life there must be another and another and another, without end, without hope—until one sees the light and elects to live by it. Yes, the struggle of the spirit is just as sharp and cruel as the combat of battle. The saints knew it, but the modern man laughs at it. Hell is whatever, wherever, one thinks it to be. If you believe you are in Hell, you are. And life, for the modern man, has become an eternal Hell for the simple reason that he has lost all hope of attaining Paradise. He does not even believe in a Paradise of his own creation. By his own thought processes he condemns himself—to the deep Freudian hell of wish fulfillment.

In that famous *Letter of the Seer* which Rimbaud wrote in his seventeenth year, a document by the way which has created more reverberations than all the writings of the masters . . . in this letter which contains the famous prescription for the poets to come, Rimbaud emphasizes that, to follow the discipline laid down, involves "ineffable torture, for which all his (the poet's) strength is needed, all his superhuman strength." In the pursuance of this discipline, he adds, the poet comes to stand forth "as the great invalid, the great criminal, the great accursed one—and the supreme savant!—for he arrives at the *unknown!*" The guarantee for this immense reward lies in the simple fact that "the poet has cultivated his soul, already richer than all others." But what happens when the poet comes to the unknown? "He ends by losing all understanding of his visions," says Rimbaud. (Which is what happened in his own case.) As though anticipating such a fate, he adds: "Still, he has seen them, hasn't he? Let him burst with his palpitations— with the unheard of, nameless things he has seen. Then let other horrible workers come after him; they will begin at the horizons where he expired."

This appeal, which had such an effect upon those to come, is noteworthy for many reasons, but chiefly because it reveals the genuine role of the poet and the true nature of tradition. Of what use the poet unless he attains to a new vision of life, unless he is willing to sacrifice his life in attesting the truth and the splendor of his vision? It is the fashion to speak of these demonic beings, these visionaries, as Romantics, to stress their subjectivity and to regard them as breaks, interruptions, stopgaps in the great stream of tradition, as though they were madmen whirling about the pivot of self. Nothing could be more untrue. It is precisely these innovators who form the links in the great chain of creative literature. One must indeed begin at the horizons where they expire—"hold the gain," as Rimbaud puts it—and not sit down comfortably in the ruins and piece together a puzzle of shards.

At the age of twelve it is said that Rimbaud's piety was so exalted that he longed for martyrdom. Three years later, in *Soleil et Chair*, he exclaims: "Flesh, marble, flower, Venus, in thee I believe!" He speaks of Aphrodite throwing upon the vast universe "infinite love in an infinite smile." And the world, he says, will answer, will vibrate "like an immense lyre in the shudder of an immense kiss." Here we see him reverting to the paganism of innocence, to that lost golden period when his life was "a banquet at which all

87

hearts opened, at which all wines flowed." It is the period of self-communion, of indescribable longing for the unknown—"*l'éblouissement de l'Infini.*" In short, the period of incubation, brief but profound, like the bliss of *samadhi.*

Another three years and, only eighteen, we find him at the end of his poetic career, writing his Last Will and Testament, so to speak. The Hell he describes so vividly he has already experienced in his soul; he is now about to live it in the flesh. What heart-rending words, in the section called "Morning," from a youth of eighteen! It is gone already, his youth, and with it all the youth of the world. His country lies prostrate and defeated; his mother wishes only to get rid of him, strange, impossible creature that he is. He has already known hunger, destitution, humiliation, rejection; he has been in prison, has witnessed the bloody Commune, perhaps even participated in it, has experienced vice and degradation, has lost his first love, has broken with his fellow artists, has surveyed the whole field of modern art and found it empty, and is now about to consign everything to the devil, himself included. And thus, thinking of his wasted youth, as later on his deathbed he will think of his whole wasted life, he asks piteously: "Had I not *once* a youth pleasant, heroic, fabulous enough to write on leaves of gold: too much luck! Through what crime, what error, have I earned my present weakness? You who maintain that some animals sob sorrowfully, that the sick despair, that the dead have bad dreams, try to tell the story of my downfall *and my slumber*.* I myself can no more explain myself than the beggar with his continual *Pater* and *Ave Maria. I no longer know how to speak.*"

He has finished the story of his own private hell . . . he is about to say good-bye. It only remains to add a few parting words. Again the image of the desert occurs—one of his most persistent images. The source of his inspiration has dried up: like Lucifer, he has "used up" the light which was given him. There remains only the lure of the beyond, the call of the deep, in answer to which he finds corroboration and completion *in life* of the dread image which haunts him: the desert. He chafes at the bit. "When will we go . . . ?" he asks. "When will we go . . . to greet the birth of the new task, the new wisdom, the flight of tyrants and demons, the end of superstition; to adore—the first ones!—Christmas on Earth?" (How reminiscent, these words, of that contemporary he never knew—Nietzsche!)

* Italics mine.

89

What revolutionary has voiced the path of duty more clearly and poignantly? What saint has used Christmas in a more divine sense? These are the words of a rebel, yes, but not of an impious one. This is a pagan, yes, but a pagan like Virgil. This is the voice of the prophet and the taskmaster, of the disciple and the initiate in one. Even the priest, idolatrous, superstitious and benighted though he be, must subscribe to *this* Christmas! "Slaves, let us not curse life!" he cries. An end to weeping and wailing, to the mortification of the flesh. An end to docility and submission, to childish beliefs and childish prayers. Away with false idols and the baubles of science. Down with dictators, demagogues, and rabble-rousers. Let us not curse life, let us worship it! The whole Christian interlude has been a denial of life, a denial of God, a denial of the Spirit. Freedom has not even been dreamed of yet. Liberate the mind, the heart, the flesh! Free the soul, that it may reign securely! This is the winter of life and "I distrust winter because it is the season of comfort!" Give us Christmas on Earth . . . not Christianity. I never was a Christian, I never belonged to *your* race. Yes, my eyes are closed to *your* light. I am a beast, a nigger . . . *but I can be saved!* You are the phony niggers, you misers, you maniacs, you fiends! I'm the real nigger and this is a nigger book. I say, let us have Christmas on Earth . . . now, *now*, do you hear? Not pie in the sky!

Thus he raves. "Thoughts out of season," indubitably.

"Ah well . . ." he seems to sigh. "Sometimes in the sky I see endless beaches covered with white and joyous nations." For a moment nothing stands between him and the certitude of dream. He sees the future as the inevitable realization of man's deepest wish. Nothing can stop it from coming, not even the phony niggers who are buggering up the world in the name of law and order. He dreams everything out to the end. All the horrible, unspeakable memories fade away. And with them all regrets. He will have his revenge yet—on the backward ones, "the friends of death." Though I go forth into the wilderness, though I make of my life a desert, though no man shall hear of me henceforth, know ye one and all that I shall be permitted to possess the truth in body and soul. You have done your utmost to disguise the truth; you have tried to destroy my soul; and in the end you will break my body on the rack . . . But I will know the truth, possess it for my own, in *this* body and with *this* soul . . .

These are the savage utterances of a seeker, a

"friend of God," even though he denies the name.

"All language being idea," said Rimbaud, "the day of the universal language will come . . . This language, the *new* or *universal*, will speak from soul to soul, resuming all perfumes, sounds, colors, linking together all thought." The key to this language, it goes without saying, is the symbol, which the creator alone possesses. It is the alphabet of the soul, pristine and indestructible. By means of it the poet, who is the lord of imagination and the unacknowledged ruler of the world, communicates, holds communion, with his fellow man. It was to establish this bridge that the youthful Rimbaud gave himself up to experiment. And how he succeeded, despite the sudden and mysterious renunciation! From beyond the grave he is still communicating, more and more powerfully as the years go on. The more enigmatic he seems, the more lucid becomes his doctrine. Paradoxical? Not at all. Whatever is prophetic can be made clear only in the time and the event. In this medium one sees backward and forward with equal clarity; communication becomes the art of establishing at any moment in time a logical and harmonious rapport between the past and the future. Any and all material makes itself available, provided it be transformed into eternal currency—the language of the soul. In this realm there are no analphabets, neither are there grammarians. It is only necessary to open the heart, to throw overboard all *literary* preconceptions . . . to stand revealed, in other words. This, of course, is tantamount to conversion. It is a radical measure, and presupposes a state of desperation. But if all other methods fail, as they inevitably do, why not this extreme measure—of conversion? It is only at the gates of hell that salvation looms. Men have failed, in every direction. Over and over they have had to retrace their steps, resume the heavy burden, begin anew the steep and difficult ascent toward the summit. Why not accept the challenge of the Spirit and yield? Why not surrender, and thus enter into a new life? The Ancient One is always waiting. Some call him the Initiator, some call him The Great Sacrifice . . .

What Rimbaud's imitators, as well as his detractors, fail to see is that he was advocating the practice of a new way of life. He was not trying to set up a new school of art, in order to divert the enfeebled spinners of words—he was pointing out the union between art and life, bridging

93

the schism, healing the mortal wound. Divine charity, that is the key to knowledge, he says. In the very beginning of *A Season in Hell* he had written: ". . . the other day, finding myself about to croak my last, I thought of seeking again the key to the banquet of old, where I might perhaps get back my appetite. *Charity is that key.*" And then he adds: "this inspiration proves that I have been dreaming!" Dreaming in hell, of course, *in that deep slumber which is unfathomable to him.* He who had "created all festivals, all triumphs, all dramas," is obliged, during his eclipse, to bury all imagination. He who had called himself mage and angel, he who had freed himself of all ties, all claims, now finds himself brought back to earth, forced to accept, to embrace, harsh reality. *Peasant,* that is what they would make of him. Returned to the country, he is to be put out of currency . . . What lies, then, had he fed on in his swollen dreams? ("In the end I will ask to be pardoned for having fed myself on lies.") But of *whom* will he ask pardon? Not of his tormentors, certainly. Not of the age which he repudiated. Not of that old goat of a mother who would put him in harness. *Of whom,* then? Let us say it—of his peers, of those who will succeed him and carry on the good fight. He is making his apologies not to us, nor even to God, but to the men of the future, the men who will greet him with open arms when we all enter the splendid cities. These are the men "of a distant race" to whom he pays allegiance and whom he regards as his true ancestors. He is removed from them only in time, not in blood or bearing. These are the men who know how to sing under torture. They are men of spirit, and to them he is linked not by antecedents—he cannot find one in the whole history of France—but by spirit. He is born in a void and he communicates with them across the void. *We* hear only the reverberations. We marvel at the sounds of this strange tongue. We know nothing of the joy and the certitude which sustained this inhuman confabulation.

What diverse spirits he has affected, altered, enslaved! What accolades he has received, and from men as different from one another in temperament, form and substance as Valéry, Claudel, André Breton. What has he in common with them? Not even his genius, for at nineteen he ransoms his genius for mysterious ends. Every act of renunciation has but one aim: the attainment of another level. (With Rimbaud, it is a drop to another level.) Only when the singer stops singing can he live his song. And if his song is defiance? Then it is violence and catastrophe. But catastrophes, as Amiel said, bring about a violent restoration of equilibrium. And Rimbaud, born under the sign of the Balance, chooses the extremes with the passion of an equilibrist.

Always it is some invisible wand, some magic star, which beckons, and then the old wisdom, the old magic, is done for. Death and transfiguration, that is the eternal song. Some seek the death they choose, whether of form, body, wisdom or soul, directly; others approach it deviously. Some accentuate the drama by disappearing from the face of the earth, leaving no clues, no traces; others make their life an even more inspiring spectacle than the confession which is their work. Rimbaud drew his death out woefully. He spread his ruin all about him, so that none could fail to comprehend the utter futility of his flight. *Anywhere, out of the world!* That is the cry of those for whom life no longer has any meaning. Rimbaud discovered the true world as a child; he tried to proclaim it as a youth; he betrayed it as a man. Forbidden access to the world of love, all his endowments were in vain. His hell did not go deep enough, he roasted in the vestibule. It was too brief a period, this season, as we know, because the rest of his life becomes a Purgatory. Did he lack the courage to swim the deep? We do not know. We know only that he surrenders his treasure—as if *it* were the burden. But the guilt which he suffered from no man escapes, not even those who are born in the light. His failure seems stupendous, though it brought him through to victory. But it is not Rimbaud who triumphs, it is the unquenchable spirit that was in him. As Victor Hugo said: "Angel is the only word in the language that cannot be worn out."

"Creation begins with a painful separation from God and the creation of an independent will to the end that this separation may be overcome in a type of unity higher than that with which the process began."*

At the age of nineteen, in the very middle of his life, Rimbaud gave up the ghost. "His Muse died at his side, among his massacred dreams," says one biographer. Nevertheless, he was a prodigy who in three years gave the impression of exhausting whole cycles of art. "It is as if he contained whole careers within himself," said Jacques Rivière. To which Matthew Josephson adds: "Indeed literature ever since Rimbaud has been engaged in the struggle to circumvent

* *The Mystic Will*, by H. H. Brinton.

him." Why? Because, as the latter says, "he made poetry *too dangerous*." Rimbaud himself declares, in the *Season*, that he "became a fabulous opera." Opera or not, he remains fabulous— nothing less. The one side of his life is just as fabulous as the other, that is the amazing thing. Dreamer and man of action, he is both at once. It is like combining in one character Shakespeare and Bonaparte. And now listen to his own words . . . "I saw that all beings are fatally attracted to happiness: action is not life, but a way of dissipating one's strength, and enervation." And then, as if to prove it, he plunges into the maelstrom. He crosses and recrosses Europe on foot, ships in one boat after another for foreign ports, is returned ill or penniless again and again; he takes a thousand and one jobs, learns a dozen or more languages, and, in lieu of dealing in words deals in coffee, spices, ivory, skins, gold, muskets, slaves. Adventure, exploration, study; association with every type of man, race, nationality; and always work, work, work, which he loathed. But above all, *ennui!* Always bored. Incurably bored. But what activity! What a wealth of experiences! *And what emptiness!* His letters to his mother are one long plaint mingled with reproaches and recriminations, with whines, entreaties and supplications. Miserable one, accursed one! Finally he becomes "the great invalid."

What is the meaning of this flight, this endless wail, this self-inflicted torture? How true, that activity is not life! Where is life, then? And which is the true reality? Certainly it cannot be this harsh reality of toil and wandering, this sordid scrimmage for possessions?

In the *Illuminations*, written in melancholy London, he had announced: *"Je suis réellement d'outre-tombe, et pas de commissions!"* That was said as poet. Now he knows it for a fact. The musician who had found something like the key of love, as he puts it, has lost the key. He has lost the key and the instrument both. Having shut all the doors, even of friendship, having burned all his bridges behind him, he will never set foot in the dominion of love. There remain only the great solitudes in the shadow of the buried tree of Good and Evil where, in his *Matinée d'ivresse*, occurs that nostalgic phrase—*"afinique nous ramenions notre très pur amour."* He wanted salvation in the form of liberty, never realizing that it comes only through surrender, through acceptance. *"Tout homme,"* said his master Baudelaire, *"que n'accepte pas les conditions de sa vie vend son âme."* With Rimbaud, creation and experience were virtually simultaneous; he

99

required only a minimum of experience to make music. As the youthful prodigy he is closer to the musician or the mathematician than the man of letters. He is born with a supersensible memory. He does not earn his creation by the sweat of his brow—it is there, on tap, waiting to be roused by the first contact with harsh reality. It is sorrow which he must cultivate, not the virtuosity of the maestro. He does not have long to wait, as we know.

He was born a seed and he remains a seed. That is the meaning of the night which surrounds him. In him there was light, a wondrous light, but it was not to shed its rays until he had perished. He came from beyond the grave, of a distant race, bringing a new spirit and a new consciousness. Does he not say—"it is wrong to say *je pense;* one should say *on me pense*"? And is it not he who says—"genius is love **and the fu**ture"? Everything he says in connection with the I of the genius is illuminating and revelatory. This one I find most significant . . . "His body is the release of which we have dreamed; the shattering of a grace thwarted by a new violence."

Let me not be accused of reading too deeply. Rimbaud meant everything he wrote "literally and in all senses," as he once explained to his mother or sister. True, he was referring then to

A Season in Hell. Nevertheless. . . . It was with him as it was with Blake and Jacob Boehme: everything they uttered was true, literal, and inspired. They dwelt in the Imagination; their dreams were realities, realities which *we* have yet to experience. "If I read myself," says Boehme, "I read God's book, and you my brothers are the alphabet which I read in myself, for my mind and will find you within me. I wish from my heart you would also find me." That last utterance voices the silent prayer which Rimbaud is constantly sending forth from the wilderness which he created for himself. The "benevolent" pride of the genius lies in his will which must be broken. The secret of deliverance lies in the practice of charity. Charity *is* the key, and Rimbaud *was* dreaming when he realized it, but the dream was reality and this reality only makes itself felt again when he is on his deathbed, when charity becomes the sweet sister which escorts him to the beyond, broken but redeemed.

During the "Night in Hell," when he realizes that he is the slave of his baptism, he cries: "O Parents, you contrived my misfortune, and your own." In the dark night of the soul, during which he proclaims himself a master in phantasmagoria and boasts that he is going to unveil every mystery, he renounces everything which would link him with the age or the land he was born in. "I am ready for perfection," he states. And he was, in a sense. He had prepared his own initiation, survived the terrible ordeal, and then relapsed into the night in which he was born. He had perceived that there was a step beyond art, he had put his foot over the threshold, and then in terror or in fear of madness he had retreated. His preparations for a new life were either insufficient or of the wrong order. Most commentators think the latter, though both are possibly true. So much emphasis has been laid upon that phrase—"long, immense, logical derangement of all the senses." So much has been said about his early debauches, about his "Bohemian" life. One forgets how utterly normal that was for a precocious youth bursting with ideas who has run away from an intolerable home atmosphere in the provinces. Rare creature that he was, he would have been abnormal had he not succumbed to the potent appeals of a city like Paris. If he was excessive in his indulgence it is only to say that the vaccination took with a vengeance. It was not such a long time he spent either in Paris or in London. Not enough to ruin a healthy lad of peasant stock. For one who was in revolt against everything it was in fact a salutary experience. The road to heaven leads through hell, does it not? To earn salvation one has to become inoculated with sin. One has to savor them all, the capital as well as the trivial sins. One has to earn death with all one's appetites, refuse no poison, reject no experience however degrading or sordid. One has to come to the end of one's forces, learn that one *is* a slave—in whatever realm—in order to desire emancipation. The perverse, negative will fostered by one's parents has to be made submissive before it can become positive and integrated with the heart and mind. The Father (in all his guises) has to be dethroned so that the Son may reign. The Father is Saturnian in every phase of his being. He is the stern taskmaster, the dead letter of the Law, the *Verboten* sign. One kicks the traces over, goes berserk, filled with a false power and a foolish pride. And then one breaks, and the I that is not the I surrenders. *But Rimbaud did not break.* He does not dethrone the Father, he identifies himself with him. He does it as much through his godlike assumption of authority as through his excesses, his ramblings, his irresponsibility. He goes over into the opposite, becomes the very enemy whom he hated. In short, he abdicates, becomes a vagabond god in search of his true kingdom. "To emasculate oneself, is not that a sure way of damning yourself?" (This is one of the many questions he poses during his agony.) And that is precisely what he does. He emasculates himself by abdicating the role for which he was chosen . . . Is it possible that in Rimbaud the sense of guilt was atrophied?

What a struggle for power, possessions, security he wages during the "active" period of his life! Did he not realize what a treasure he possessed, what power he wielded, what unimpeachable security he knew when he was simply the poet? (I wish I could say that he also revealed himself to be the poet of action, but the accidents which stud the latter half of his life never develop into those incidents which profit the man of action.) No, there is a blindness which it is impossible to fathom, and Rimbaud's is that sort. A curse has been laid on him. He not only loses his sense of direction, but he loses his touch. Everything goes wrong. He changes identity so thoroughly that if he were to pass himself on the road he would not recognize himself. This is perhaps the last desperate way of tricking madness—to become so utterly sane that one does not know one is insane. Rimbaud never lost contact with reality; on the contrary, he embraced it like a fiend. What he did was to forsake the true reality of his being. No wonder that he was bored to death. He could not possibly live with himself, since that self was in forfeit. In this respect one is reminded of Lautréamont's words: "I go on existing, like basalt! In the middle, as in the beginning of life, angels resemble themselves: how long it has been since I ceased to resemble myself!"

One has the feeling that in Abyssinia he even tried to amputate the organ of memory. But toward the end, when he has become "the great invalid," when to the accompaniment of a hand organ he takes up the thread of his stifled dreams, the memories of the past well up. What a pity we have no record of the strange language he indulged in on the hospital bed, his leg gone, a huge tumor blossoming on his thigh, the insidious cancer germs roving through his body like plundering marauders. Dreams and hallucinations vie with one another in an endless fugue— and no audience but the devout sister who is praying for his soul. Now the dreams he dreamed and the dreams he lived interfuse; the spirit, at last freed of its fetters, makes music again.

His sister has attempted to give us an inkling of these unrecorded melodies. She remarks, if I remember rightly, upon their supernal quality. They were not, we are led to believe, like either the poems or the illuminations. They were all that plus something else, plus that something,

105

perhaps, which Beethoven gave us in the last quartets. He had not lost the master's touch; with the approach of death he was even more the genius than he was in his youth. They are fugues now not of clashing, discordant phrases however illuminated, but of essences and quintessences garnered through the struggle with the sternest demon of all, Life. Experience and imagination now blend to form a chant which is a gift and not a curse or a malediction. It is no longer *his* music, *his* magistry. The ego has been routed, the song and the instrument become one. It is his oblation on the altar of dethroned pride. It is the Apocatastasis. Creation is no longer arrogance, defiance, or vanity, but play. He can play now on his deathbed as he can pray, for his work as a sufferer is ended. The keel of his ship has at last burst asunder, he is going to the sea. Perhaps in these last hours he understands the true purpose of human toil, that it is slavery when linked to blind or selfish ends and joy when it is performed in the service of mankind.

There is no joy like the joy of the creator, for creation has no other end than creation. "Let us refine our fingers, that is, *all* our points of contact with the external world," he once urged. In the same sense God refines His fingers—when he elevates man to the level of creation. The thrill of creation is felt throughout all creation. All forms, all orders of being from the angels to the worms, are struggling to communicate with those above and below. No efforts are lost, no music goes unheard. But in every misuse of power not only is God wounded but Creation itself is halted and Christmas on Earth postponed that much longer.

> "Ah! je n'aurai plus d'envie:
> Il s'est chargé de ma vie.
>
> Salut à lui chaque fois
> Que chante le coq gaulois."

I transpose these couplets deliberately in the same spirit that I once mistakenly translated *"il"* as *Dieu*. I cannot help but believe that the fatal attraction to *le bonheur* which Rimbaud spoke of means the joy of finding God. *Alors—"Salut à Lui chaque fois que . . ."*

Why is it, I ask myself, that I adore Rimbaud above all other writers? I am no worshipper of adolescence, neither do I pretend to myself that he is as great as other writers I might mention. But there is something in him that touches me as the work of no other man does. And I come to him through the fogs of a language I have never mastered! Indeed, it was not until I foolishly tried to translate him that I began to properly estimate the strength and the beauty of his utterances. In Rimbaud I see myself as in a mirror. Nothing he says is alien to me, however wild, absurd or difficult to understand. To understand one has to surrender, and I remember distinctly making that surrender the first day I glanced at his work. I read only a few lines that day, a little over ten years ago, and trembling like a leaf I put the book away. I had the feeling then, and I have it still, that he had said *all* for our time. It was as though he had put a tent over the void. He is the only writer whom I have read and reread with undiminished joy and excitement, always discovering something new in him, always profoundly touched by his purity. Whatever I say of him will always be tentative, nothing more than an approach—at best an *aperçu*. He is the one writer whose genius I envy; all the others, no matter how great, never arouse my jealousy. And he was finished at nineteen! Had I read Rimbaud in my youth I doubt that I would ever have written a line. How fortunate sometimes is our ignorance!

Until I ran across Rimbaud it was Dostoievsky

who reigned supreme. In one sense he always will, just as Buddha will always be dearer to me than Christ. Dostoievsky went to the very bottom, remained there an immeasurable time, and emerged a whole man. I prefer the whole man. And if I must live only once on this earth, then I prefer to know it as Hell, Purgatory and Paradise all in one. Rimbaud experienced a Paradise, but it was premature. Still, because of that experience, he was able to give us a more vivid picture of Hell. His life as a man, though he was never a mature man, was a Purgatory. But that is the lot of most artists. What interests me extremely in Rimbaud is his vision of Paradise regained, Paradise *earned*. This, of course, is something apart from the splendor and the magic of his words, which I consider incomparable. What defeats me is his life, which is at such utter variance with his vision. Whenever I read his life I feel that I too have failed, that all of us fail. And then I go back to his words—and they never fail.

Why is it then that I now adore him above all other writers? Is it because his failure is so instructive? Is it because he resisted until the very last? I admit it, I love all those men who are called rebels and failures. I love them because they are so human, so "human—all-too-human."

We know that God too loves them above all others. Why? Is it because they are the proving ground of the spirit? Is it because they are the sacrificed ones? How Heaven rejoices when the prodigal son returns! Is this an invention of man's or of God's? I believe that here man and God see eye to eye. Man reaches upward, God reaches downward; sometimes their fingers touch.

When I am in doubt as to whom I love more, those who resist or those who surrender, I know that they are one and the same. One thing is certain, God does not want us to come to Him in innocence. We are to know sin and evil, we are to stray from the path, to get lost, to become defiant and desperate: we are to resist as long as we have the strength to resist, in order that the surrender be complete and abject. It is our privilege as free spirits to elect for God with eyes wide-open, with hearts brimming over, with a desire that outweighs all desires. The innocent one! God has no use for him. He is the one who "plays at Paradise for eternity." To become ever more conscious, ever more gravid with knowledge, to become more and more burdened with guilt—that is man's privilege. No man is free of guilt; to whatever level one attains one is beset with new responsibilities, new sins. In destroying man's innocence God converted man into a potential ally. Through reason and will He gave him the power of choice. And man in his wisdom always chooses God.

I spoke a while back of Rimbaud's preparations for a new life, meaning of course the life of the spirit. I would like to say a little more about this, to add that not only were these preparations insufficient and of the wrong sort but that he was the victim of a grave misunderstanding as to the nature of his role. Had he known a different spiritual climate his life might well have taken a different course. Had he ever encountered a Master he would never have made a martyr of himself. He was ready for quite a different sort of adventure than the one he experienced. And in another sense he was not ready, because, as the saying goes, when the pupil is ready the Master is always there. The trouble was that he would acknowledge *"ni Maître, ni Dieu."* He was in dire need of help, but his pride was inordinate. Rather than humble himself, rather than bend, he flings himself to the dogs. That he could only remain intact by renouncing his calling is a tribute to his purity but also a condemnation of the age. I think of Boehme, who was a cobbler, who did not have a language, we might say, but who forged one for himself and with it, baffling as it may be to the uninitiated, communicated his message to the world. It may be said of course that by abruptly silencing his voice Rimbaud also succeeded in communicating, but such was not his intention. He despised the world which wanted to acclaim him, he denied that his work had any value. But this has only one meaning—that he wanted to be taken at face value! If one wishes to read deeper into this act of renunciation, then one can compare it with Christ's and say that he chose his martyrdom in order to give it everlasting significance. But Rimbaud chose unconsciously. It was those who had need of him, those whom he despised, who gave his work *and* his life meaning. Rimbaud simply threw up his hands. He was not prepared to accept responsibility for his utterances, knowing that he could not be accepted at face value.

It is not strange that the Nineteenth Century is constellated with demonic figures. One has only to think of Blake, de Nerval, Kierkegaard, Lautréamont, Strindberg, Nietzsche, Dostoievsky—all tragic figures, and tragic in a new sense. All of them are concerned with the problem of the soul, with the expansion of consciousness and the creation of new moral values. At the hub of this wheel which sheds light on the void,

Blake and Nietzsche reign like dazzling twin stars; their message is still so new that we think of them in terms of insanity.* Nietzsche rearranges all existent values; Blake fashions a new cosmogony. Rimbaud is close to both in many ways. He is like a nova which appears suddenly, grows to terrifying brilliance, then plunges to earth. ("Et je vécus, étincelle d'or de la lumière *nature*.") In the darkness of the womb, which he sought with the same ferocity as he did the light of heaven, he transforms into radium. His is a substance which it is dangerous to handle; his is a light which annihilates when it does not exalt or illumine. As a star he hovered too close to the earth's orbit. Not content to shed his brilliance *over* the earth, he was fatally attracted by the reflection of his own image in the dead mirror of life. He wanted to transform his light into radiant power; this could only be accomplished by a fall. This delusion, which Orientals call ignorance rather than sin, emphasizes the confusion between the domains of art and of life which gripped the men of the Nineteenth Century. All the great spirits of the modern age have struggled to demagnetize themselves, as it were. All were annihilated by Jovian bolts. They

* "Let us be happy! I am God, and I have made this caricature." (Nietzsche from the asylum.)

113

were like inventors who, having discovered electricity, knew nothing about insulation. They were attuned to a new power which was breaking through, but their experiments led to disaster.

All these men, and Rimbaud was one of them, were inventors, lawgivers, warriors, prophets. They *happened* to be poets. The superabundance of their talents, coupled with the fact that the age was not ripe for their coming, combined to create an ambiance of defeat and frustration. In a profound sense they were usurpers, and the fate meted out to them reminds us of the suffering of the protagonists in the ancient Greek dramas. They were pursued and laid low by the Furies which, in modern parlance, are the insanities. Such is the price man pays when he attempts to elevate the magical level of his gods, when he attempts to live in accordance with the new code before the new gods are securely entrenched. These gods, of course, are always the projection of man's exalted inner powers. They represent the magical element in creation; they blind and intoxicate because they rend the darkness from which they spring. Baudelaire expressed it out of the depths of his own bitter experience when he said: "*En effet il est défendu à l'homme, sous peine de déchéance et de mort intellectuelle, de déranger les conditions primordiales de son*

*existence et de rompre l'équilibre de ses facultés
avec les milieux où elles sont destinées à se mou-
voir, de déranger son destin pour y substituer une
fatalité d'un genre nouveau . . ."*

In brief, the dreamer should be content to
dream, confident that "imagination makes substance." This is the poet's function, the highest
because it brings him to the unknown—to the
limits of creation. The masters are beyond the
spell of creation; they function in the pure white
light of being. They are done with becoming;
they have incorporated themselves in the heart
of creation, fully realized as men and luminous
with the glow of the divine essence. They have
transfigured themselves to the point where they
have only to radiate their divinity.

The elect, being adepts, are at home anywhere. They know the meaning of hell but they
do not localize it, not even as earthly existence.
They are devachanees; they enjoy the intervals
between one state of existence and another. But
the free spirits, who are the tormented ones—
born out of time and out of rhythm—can only
interpret their intermediary states as hell itself.
Rimbaud was such a one. The excruciating boredom from which he suffered was the reflection
of the vacuum in which he existed—whether he
created it or not is immaterial. One thing seems

clear, in this connection: he could put his powers to no use. This is a partial truth, to be sure, but it is this aspect of truth which the man of culture is concerned with. It is the truth of history, so to speak. And history tends more and more to be identified as man's fate.

Now and then, from the deep, hidden river of life, great spirits in human form are thrown up; like semaphores in the night they warn of danger ahead. But their appeal is in vain to those "abandoned but still burning locomotives" (the false spirits of the age) "who hold to the rails for a time." The culture of these souls, said Rimbaud, whose image I use, *began with accidents*. It is this atmosphere of accident and catastrophe which permeates the historical level of interpretation. The demonic figures, possessed because they are imbued with a passion beyond them, are the sentinels who appear from nowhere in the darkest hours of night. Theirs is the voice which goes unheeded.

The bogs of Western culture which await the derailed *trains de luxe* in which our pompous spirits sit blithely bombinating their stale aphorisms Rimbaud described vividly. "I see that my discomforts come from my failure to understand soon enough that we are of the Western World. The marshes of the West!" Then quickly he adds: *"Non que je croie la lumière alterée, la forme extenuée, le mouvement égaré . . ."* (He is not the dupe of history, one observes.) In the next breath, as if he knew his fate from eternity, he is saying: *"L'esprit est autorité, il veut que je sois en Occident."*

Now and then, during his sojourn in the lower depths, he remarks, quite as though he were stirring in his sleep—*"C'est la vie encore!"* Yes, life it is, no mistake about it. Only it is the other side of that double-faced coin. And he who, however mockingly he phrases it, is nevertheless in possession of the truth, must put up with it, must see it through. There will be no other life for him . . . he chose it from beyond the grave. All the elements of his character were laid down at birth; they will lend to his destiny the unique character of his agony. He will suffer not only because his parents willed it, not only because the age demanded that he suffer, he will suffer because of the whole evolution through which the spirit of man has gone. He will suffer precisely because it is the spirit of man which is in travail. He will suffer as only the seed suffers when it falls upon barren ground.

In the light of these reflections, why should the second half of his life appear more mysterious and enigmatic than the first? Is a man's destiny not determined by his character? We become what we are, else all is the play of hazard. The fortuitous *rencontres*, the strange accidents of fortune, make sublime sense. A man is always consistent with himself, even when at some unforeseen moment in an otherwise commendable life he suddenly commits a horrible crime. It is so often, is it not, the man of exemplary character who commits the nauseating crime.

Rimbaud repeatedly calls attention to his bad traits. He underscores them, in fact. When I spoke earlier of the latter half of his life being a Calvary, I meant it in the sense that he gave his impulses free rein. He is crucified not because of his exceptional qualities, for they would have borne him through any ordeal, but because he surrenders to his instincts. For Rimbaud this surrender spells abdication: the ungovernable steeds take over the reins. What work it is now to find the right track! Endless work. Sometimes it would seem that he is not so much a *different* man as a man at loose ends. The poet will still manifest himself, if only in the bizarre pattern of his erratic tracks. Look at the places he allows himself to be dragged to! He is in and out of almost every European port, headed now this way, now that—Cyprus, Norway, Egypt, Java, Arabia, Abyssinia. Think of his pursuits, his studies, his speculations! All marked "exotic." His exploits are as daring and unchartered as his poetic flights. His life is never prosaic, however dull or painful it may appear to him . . . He was in the midst of life, thinks the clerk in his office. Yes, many a solid citizen, to say nothing of the poets, would give an arm or a leg could they but imitate Rimbaud's adventurous life. The pathologist may call it "ambulatory paranoia," but to the stay-at-home it seems like bliss. To the Frenchman cultivating his garden it must, of course, have seemed like sheer dementia. It must have been terrifying, this *tour du monde* on an empty stomach. It must have seemed even more crazy, more terrifying, when they learned that he was getting dysentery from constantly carrying in his belt 40,000 francs in gold. Whatever he did was bizarre, fantastic, *inoui*. His itinerary is one uninterrupted phantasmagoria. Yes, there are the passionate and imaginative elements in it which we admire in his writing, no question about that. But there is also a coldness about his acts, just as there was in his behavior as a poet. Even in his poetry there is this cold fire, this light without warmth. This is an element which his mother donated and which she aggravates by her attitude toward him. To her he is always unpredictable, the dismal sport of a loveless marriage. No matter how he struggles to remove himself from the parental orbit, she is there like a lodestone pulling him back. He can free himself from the claims of the literary world but never from the mother. She is the black star which attracts him fatally. Why did he not forget about her utterly, as he did all the others? Evidently she is the link with the past which he cannot relinquish. She becomes, in fact, *the past*. His father had the wanderlust too, it seems, and finally, just after Rimbaud was born, he wandered away forever. But the son, no matter how far he wanders, cannot make this break; he takes the father's place, and like the father whom he identifies himself with, he continues to add to his mother's misery. And so he wanders. He wanders and wanders until he reaches the land of the shepherds "where the zebus dream, buried in grass up to the dew-laps." There he too dreams, I am certain, but whether they are glorious or bitter dreams we do not know. He no longer puts them down; he gives us only the marginal notes—instructions, requests, demands, complaints. Had he reached the point where it was no longer necessary to record his dreams? Was action the substitute? These questions will be asked eternally. One thing alone is evident—he knew no joy. He was still possessed, still driven.

He does not abandon the creator's task in order to bask in the light. He is all energy, but it is not the energy of a being "whose center is at rest."*

Wherein lies the enigma, then? Not in his outward behavior, certainly, for even as a freak he is consistent with himself. Even when he dreams of one day having a son, a son who might become an engineer (sic), we can follow him. To be sure, the idea is a bit *bouleversante,* but we can swallow it. Has he not prepared us to expect *anything* of him? Is he not human too? Has he not a right to play with notions of marriage, fatherhood and the like? The poet who can go elephant hunting, who can write home for a "Theoretical and Practical Manual of Exploration," who can dream of submitting a paper on the Gallas to the Geographical Society, what is so startling if he also craves a white wife and a child after his own heart? People wonder that he treated his Abyssinian mistress so decently. And why not, pray? Is it so strange that he should be civil, polite, even considerate . . . that he should now and then do a little good, as he puts it? Let us remember Shylock's speech!

No, what is difficult to swallow, what sticks like a lump in the throat, is his renunciation of

* "The difficulty now is to get rid of me," said Nietzsche from the asylum. Signed "The Crucified One."

art. This is where Monsieur Tout-le-monde comes in. This is his *crime,* as we like to say. All his faults, his vices, his excesses we can pardon —but not this. This is the unforgivable affront, *n'est-ce pas?* How we betray ourselves here! We would all like to run out sometimes, wouldn't we? We are fed up, sick of the whole works, but we stick. We stick because we lack the courage, the imagination to follow suit. We don't stick it out of a sense of solidarity. Ah no! Solidarity is a myth—in this age, at least. Solidarity is for slaves who wait until the world becomes one huge wolf pack . . . then they will pounce all at once, all together, and rip and rend like envious beasts. Rimbaud was a lone wolf. He did not, however, slink out by the back door with his tail between his legs. No, nothing of the sort. He thumbed his nose at Parnassus—and at the judges, priests, schoolmasters, critics, slave drivers, moneybags and mountebanks who make up our distinguished cultural society. (Don't flatter yourself that his age was any worse than ours! Don't think for a moment that these misers, maniacs and hyenas, these phony ones on every level, are now extinct! This is *your* problem as well as his!) No, as I say, he wasn't worried about not being accepted . . . he despised the petty satisfactions which most of us crave. He saw that it was all a stinking mess, that being another historical cipher would get him nowhere. He wanted to live, he wanted more room, more freedom: he wanted to express himself, no matter how. And so he said, *"Fuck you, Jack! Fuck you one and all!"* Whereupon he opened his fly and pissed on the works—and from a considerable height, as Céline once put it. And that, dear slaves of life, is really unpardonable, is it not? *That is the crime,* isn't it? Very well, let us pronounce the verdict. "Rimbaud, you have been judged guilty. You will have your head neatly cut off in a public place in the name of the discontented artists of the civilized world." At this moment, when I think of the glee with which the mob always rushes to the guillotine, especially when there is a "choice" victim, I recall the words of "The Stranger" in Albert Camus' novel—and I know what it is to be an alien soul. The *procureur* has just put to the audience attending the trial of this "monster" the rhetorical question: *"A-t-il seulement exprimé des regrets? Jamais, messieurs. Pas une seule fois au cours de l'instruction cet homme n'a paru ému de son abominable forfait."* (This is always the real crime, notice . . . never the crime itself.) And so, at this point, the victim continues his interior monologue. . . . *"A ce moment, il s'est tourné vers moi et m'a désigné du doigt en continuant à m'accabler sans qu'en réalité je comprenne bien pourquoi. Sans doute je ne pouvais pas m'empêcher de reconnaître qu'il avait raison. Je ne regrettais pas beaucoup mon acte. Mais tant d'acharnement m'étonnait. J'aurais voulu essayer de lui expliquer cordialement, presque avec affection, que je n'avais jamais pu regretter vraiment quelque chose. J'étais toujours pris par ce qui allait arriver, par aujourd'hui ou par demain. Mais naturellement, dans l'état où l'on m'avait mis, je ne pouvais parler à personne sur ce ton. Je n'avais pas le droit de me montrer affectueux, d'avoir de la bonne volonté. Et j'ai essayé d'écouter encore parce que le procureur s'est mis à parler de mon âme."*

In the section of *Clowns and Angels* called "The Poet's Creation," Wallace Fowlie puts his finger on that superlative aspect of Rimbaud's being which sets him apart, which marks, in my opinion, the heroism of the poet. "The genius," he writes, "is both the master of silence and its slave. The poet exists not only in the words to which he signs his name, but he is also in the whiteness which remains on the page. His honesty is his intactness, and Rimbaud gloriously lived intact."

It is curious to note how Rimbaud himself employs this word "intact." *"Les criminels dégoutent comme des chatrés; moi, je suis intact, et ça m'est égal."* He sees the master and the slave, the judge and the criminal, the rebel and the conformer held by the same yoke: this is their Hell, to be yoked to one another under the delusion that they differ one from the other. The poet is in the same predicament, he implies. He too is bound; his spirit is not free, his imagination cannot soar unfettered. Rimbaud therefore refuses to revolt, he renounces. Though he had not intended it, it was the surest way to make his influence felt. By maintaining a resolute silence he makes his presence felt. This comes close to resembling the technique of the sage.* It is more effective than cannonades. Instead of becoming another voice, the poet thus becomes *the* voice—the voice of the silence.

While you are in the world and part of it, say your say, then shut your trap forever more! But don't capitulate, don't bend! The penalty? Ejection. Self-ejection, since one has already rejected the world. Is it such a terrible fate? Only if one aspires to the light of fame. There must be those, too, who reign in silence and in darkness. The world is composed of dualities, in the spiritual

* Did not Lao-tse attempt the same thing?

as well as the physical realm. Evil has just as great a place as good, darkness as light. Shadow and substance always. To the man of God it is the twilight world which is uninhabitable, for this is the realm of confusion. It was in this zone that Nietzsche situated the fallen gods. In this realm neither God nor Satan is recognizable. This is the valley of death which the spirit traverses, the dark interval during which man loses his relation with the cosmos. It is also "the time of the Assassins." Men no longer vibrate with exaltation; they writhe and squirm with envy and hate. Having no armature they know nothing of ascension; acknowledging no tension, they merely react. The medieval man recognized the Prince of Darkness and paid just homage to the powers of evil, as is evident from the testimony of stone and script. But the man of the Middle Ages also recognized and acknowledged God. His life therefore was keen and rich, it sounded the full gamut. By contrast, the life of the modern man is pale and empty. The terrors he knows exceed any known to the men of previous ages, for he lives in the world of the unreal, surrounded by phantoms. He has not even the possibilities of joy or deliverance which were open to the slaves of the ancient world. He has become the victim of his own inner emptiness; his torments are the torments of sterility. Amiel, who knew the age so well and who was also a "victim" of it, has given us an account of "the sterility of genius." This is one of the most alarming phrases that man can utter. It means the end is in sight . . .

Speaking of the end, I cannot help recalling Amiel's words when referring to the repugnance which Taine's style aroused in him. "It excites no feeling whatever; it is simply a means of information. I imagine this kind of thing will be the literature of the future—a literature *à l'américaine,* as different as possible from Greek art, giving us algebra instead of life, the formula instead of the image, the exhalations of the crucible instead of the divine madness of Apollo. Cold vision will replace the joys of thought, and we shall see the death of poetry, flayed and dissected by science."

In the case of a suicide we do not concern ourselves with whether he died a quick or a lingering death, whether his agony was great or little. It is the *act* which has importance for us, for suddenly we are made to realize that to be and not to be are acts—not intransitive verbs!— which make existence and death synonymous. The act of the suicide always has a detonating effect; it shocks us for a moment into awareness. It makes us realize that *we* are blind and dead. How typical of our sick-ridden world that the law should view such attempts with hypocritical severity! We don't want to be reminded of what we have left undone; we cower at the thought that from beyond the grave the finger of the escaped one will be forever pointed at us.

Rimbaud was a *living* suicide. All the more unbearable for us! In decency he might have ended it at nineteen, but no, he dragged it out, he made us witness, through the folly of a wasted life, the living death which we are all inflicting upon ourselves. He caricatured his own grandeur, so that we might revile our puny efforts the more. He toiled like a nigger, so that we might revel in the life of slavery which we have adopted. All the qualities which he displayed in the eighteen year struggle with life were qualities which make, as we say today, "for success." That he should have made of success such a bitter failure was his triumph. It required diabolical courage (even if it was unwitting) to make that proof demonstrable. When we pity the suicide we pity ourselves, really, for lacking the courage to follow his example. We cannot abide too many defections from the ranks—we would be demoralized. What we want are victims of life to keep us company in our misery. We know each other so well, too well; we disgust one another. But we continue to observe the conventional politeness of worms. We try to do it even when we are exterminating one another . . . Familar words, these, are they not? They will be repeated to us by Lawrence, by Céline, by Malaquais—and by others. And those who use these words will be reviled as renegades, as escapists, as rats who desert the sinking ship. (As if the rats did not show supreme intelligence!) But the ship *is* sinking, there are no two ways about that. Lawrence tells about it in his war letters, and again in writing of *Moby Dick* . . . *On va où l'on pèse,* declares St. Exupéry in the exalted pages of his *Pilote de Guerre.*

We're on the way, no doubt about that. But where is the Ark which will carry us through the Flood? And of what materials will it be made? As for the chosen ones, they will unquestionably have to be made of different fiber than the men who made *this* world. We are coming to the end, and it is a catastrophic end which we face. Warnings communicated by word have long ceased to move us. Acts are demanded, suicidal acts perhaps, but acts fraught with meaning.

Rimbaud's gesture of renunciation was such an act. It leavened literature. Will it leaven life? I doubt it. I doubt if anything will stem the tide which threatens to engulf us. But there is one thing his coming did achieve—it transformed those of us who are still sentient, still alive to the future, into "arrows of longing for the other shore."

The important thing about death, for man, is that he is able to distinguish it from dissolution. Man dies *for* something, if he dies at all. The order and harmony which sprang from primordial chaos, as the myths tell us, infuse our lives with a purpose which is beyond us, a purpose to which we sacrifice ourselves when we achieve awareness. This sacrifice is made on the altar of creation. What we create with hand and tongue is nothing; it is what we create with our lives that counts. It is only when we make ourselves a part of creation that we begin to live.

It is not death which challenges us at every step but life. We have honored the death-eaters *ad nauseam,* but what of those who accept the challenge of life? In what way do we honor these? From Lucifer to Anti-Christ there runs a flame of passion which man will always honor as long as he is mere man; it is against this passion, which is the flame of life, that we must oppose the serene acceptance of the enlightened ones.

One must pass through the flame in order to know death and embrace it. The strength of the rebel, who is the Evil One, lies in his inflexibility, but true strength lies in submission which permits one to dedicate his life, through devotion, to something beyond himself. The strength of the one leads to isolation, which is castration, while the strength of the other leads to unification, which is lasting fertility.

But passion always has its *raison d'être*, and the passion of the creator, which makes his life on earth a Calvary, has its higher octave in the passion of a Christ who incarnates all human suffering. The poet's passion is the result of his vision, of his ability to see life in its essence and its wholeness. Once this vision is shattered or deranged, passion dribbles away. In the realm of art we are definitely approaching the end of passion. Though we still turn out productive giants, their works lie like fallen tombstones amidst the still intact, still upright splendors of ancient times. Despite all its powers, society can not sustain the artist if it is impervious to the *vision* of the artist. For a long time now our society has been thoroughly uninterested in the message of the artist. The voice which goes unheeded eventually becomes silent. For the anarchy of society the artist answers with anaudia.

Rimbaud was the first to make the gesture. His example has cast a spell on us. Let us not look for his disciples among the literary figures of our time, let us seek them rather in the obscure, eclipsed ones, among the young who are forced to stifle their genius. Let us look first of all to our own country, America, where the toll is heaviest. In this new form of protest we assist at the destruction of the egg. This is the surest way to undermine the tottering edifice of a rotten society. Its effects are more swift and lasting than the havoc wrought by Super-fortresses. If the poet is to have no place, no share, in the birth of a new order then he will blast it at the very core. This threat is not imaginary; it is actual. It is the prelude to a dance of death more terrible far than that of the Middle Ages.

The only creative spirits in modern times were the demonic beings; in them was focussed the passion which is dribbling away. They had rediscovered the source of life, that banquet of old at which Rimbaud sought to restore his appetite, but their means of communication were cut off. *Men no longer communicate*, that is the tragedy of modern times. Society has long since ceased to be a community; it has broken up into aggregations of helpless atoms. That which alone can unite it—the presence and worship of God—is missing.

When, in his extreme youth, Rimbaud chalked up on the doors of the churches *"Death to God!"* he proved himself to be closer to God than the powers who rule the Church. His arrogance and defiance were never directed against the poor, the unfortunate, the truly devout; he was fighting the usurpers and pretenders, fighting all that was false, vain, hypocritical and life-destroying. He wanted the earth to re-become the Paradise which it was, which it still is beneath the veil of illusion and delusion. He was utterly uninterested in a ghostly Paradise situated in a mythical beyond. Here and now, in the flesh, as members of one great community fired with life—that was how he envisaged Christmas on Earth.

"On meurt pour cela dont on peut vivre." These are not his words, but the meaning is his. Death lies in separation, in living apart. It does not mean simply to cease being. A life which has no significance here below will have none in the hereafter. Rimbaud, I believe, understood this clearly. He gave up the struggle on one level to resume it on another. His renunciation was in this sense an affirmation. He realized that only in silence and darkness could the ingredients of art be restored. He followed the laws of his being

133

to the end, shattering all forms, his own included. At the very beginning of his career he understood what others only understand at the end, if at all, that the sacred word no longer has validity. He realized that the poison of culture had transformed beauty and truth into artifice and deception. He takes Beauty on his knee and he finds her bitter. He abandons her. It is the only way he can still honor her. What is it again that he says in the depths of hell? *"Des erreurs qu'on me souffle: magies, faux parfums, musique puérile."* (For me this is the most haunting, baffling line in the *Season*.) When he boasted that he possessed all talents, he meant—*on this phony level!* Or—with this "lying cultural mask." In this realm he was, of course, a master. But this is the realm of confusion, the *Mamser* world. Here everything is of equal value and therefore of no value. Do you want me to whistle? Do you want a *danse de ventre*? Okay! Anything you wish. Just name it!

Everything that Rimbaud voiced in his writings proclaimed this truth, that "we live not in the midst of facts, but of profundities and symbols." The mystery which inheres in his writing permeates his life. We cannot *explain* his actions, we can only permit them to reveal what we long to know. He was as much a mystery to himself as to others, as much mystified by his own utterances as by his subsequent life in the world. He sought the outside world as a refuge. A refuge from what? Perhaps from the terrors of lucidity. He is like a saint in reverse. With him the light comes first, then the knowledge and experience of sin. Sin is a mystery to him; he has to put it on, as the penitents of old adopted the hair shirt.

He ran away, we say. But perhaps he ran *toward* something. It is obvious that he avoided one kind of madness only to become the victim of another. He squeezes out of exits like a man struggling with a strait jacket. No sooner has one tragedy been averted than another besets him. He is a marked man. "They" are after him. His poetic flights, which are like progressive stages in an interrupted trance, had their parallel in the senseless flights which rushed him headlong from one corner of the world to another. How often he is brought back crushed and defeated! He rests just long enough to be repaired —like a cruiser or a long range bomber. Ready for action again. Zoom! He is off, flying toward the sun. It is light he seeks—and human warmth. His illuminations seem to have drained him of all natural warmth; in his blood is a glacial thaw. But the farther he flies the darker it gets. The earth is enveloped in blood and darkness. The ice caps move in toward the center.

It was his destiny, it seems, to have wings and to be chained to the earth. He strains as if to make the outermost stars, only to find himself wallowing in the mud. Indeed, the more he flaps his wings, the deeper he finds himself imprisoned in the earth. In him fire and air war with water and earth. He is an eagle chained to a rock. The little birds are the ones which eat his heart out.

His time was not yet. Too soon, this vision of Christmas on Earth! Too early, the hope of abolishing false gods, crude superstitions, cheap panaceas. The race of this earth has a long period of travail ahead before emerging into the white light of dawn. *Dawn* is a pregnant word with him . . . In his heart Rimbaud seems to have understood. We should never interpret his tremendous desire for liberty—it is the desire of a doomed man!—as a wish for his own personal salvation.* He speaks for the race of Adam which knew eternal life but exchanged it for the knowledge which is death. His pagan zeal is the fervor of a soul which remembers its origins. He is not seeking a return to Nature, à la Rousseau. Far from it. He is seeking grace. Had he

* "I must have beings who resemble me!" said Lautréamont.

been able to believe, he would have surrendered his soul long ago. It was his heart which was paralyzed. Those duologues which he held with his sister at the hospital resume not only the question which held him in suspense all his life but the quest. She believes so sincerely and implicitly, why can't he? Are they not of the same blood? He no longer asks *why* she believes, only —*do you?* This is the final leap for which he has to muster all his strength. It is the leap out of himself, the bursting of the bonds. It is no longer important now *what* he believes in, only—*to believe*. In one of those alternations of mood which characterize the *Season in Hell*, after an exalted outburst in which he maintains that reason is born in him again, that he sees the world is good, blesses life, loves his fellowman, he adds: *"Ce ne sont plus des promesses d'enfance. Ni l'espoir d'échapper à la vieillesse et à la mort. Dieu fait ma force et je loue Dieu."* This God who is man's strength is neither a Christian god nor a pagan god. He is simply God. He is accessible to all men of whatever race, breed or culture. He may be found in any place at any time, without benefit of mediation. He is Creation itself and will continue to exist whether man believes or not.

But the more creative a man is, the more certain he is to recognize his Maker. Those who resist most stoutly merely testify the more to His existence. The struggle against is as valiant as the struggle for; the difference lies in the fact that the one who struggles against has his back to the light. He is fighting his own shadow. It is only when this shadow play exhausts him, when finally he falls prostrate, that the light which sweeps over him can reveal to him the splendors which he had mistaken for phantoms. This is the surrender of pride and egotism which is demanded of all, great or small.

An artist earns the right to call himself a creator only when he admits to himself that he is but an instrument. "Author, creator, poet! That man has not yet existed." Thus spake Rimbaud in the arrogance of youth. But he was voicing a profound truth. Man creates nothing of and by himself. All is created, all has been foreseen . . . and yet there is freedom. Freedom to sing God's praises. This is the highest performance man can enact; when he acts thus he takes his place by the side of his Creator. This is his liberty and salvation, since it is the only way to say Yea to life. God wrote the score, God conducts the orchestra. Man's role is to make music with his own body. Heavenly music, *bien entendu*, for all else is cacophony.

No sooner had the cadaver been shipped home than Rimbaud's mother slipped off to arrange the funeral obsequies. His withered, mutilated body riddled with the marks of his agonies is shovelled under in jig time. It was as though she were ridding herself of the pest. She probably fumigated the house on her return from the cemetery whither she and his sister Isabelle had followed the hearse: these two, no more, composed the cortège. Rid of the "genius" at last, Madame Rimbaud could now devote herself in peace to the animals and the crops, to the petty rounds of her petty provincial life.

What a mother! The very incarnation of stupidity, bigotry, pride and stubbornness. Whenever the harassed genius threatened to accommodate himself to his hell, whenever his tormented spirit flagged, she was there to jab him with the pitchfork or pour a bit of burning oil on his wounds. It was she who thrust him out into the world, she who denied him, betrayed him, persecuted him. She even robbed him of that privilege which every Frenchman craves— the pleasure of having a good funeral.

The body finally delivered up to the worms, Rimbaud returns to the dark kingdom, there to search for his true mother. In life he knew only this witch, this harridan from whose loins he sprang like the missing wheel of a clock. His revolt from her tyranny and stupidity converted him into a solitary. His affective nature completely maimed, he was forever incapable of giving or receiving love. He knew only how to oppose will to will. At best he knew pity, never love.

In his youth we see him as a zealot, a fanatic. No compromise. Only the *volte-face*. As the revolutionary, he seeks desperately for an ideal society in which he can staunch the wound of separation. This is the mortal wound from which he never recovers. He becomes an absolutist, since nothing can bridge the void between the actual and the ideal but a perfection in which all error and falsity are swallowed up. Only perfection can blot out the memory of a wound which runs deeper than the river of life.

Incapable of adapting or of integrating, he seeks endlessly—only to discover that it is *not* here, *not* there, *not* this, *not* that. He learns the not-ness of everything. His defiance remains the one positive thing in the void of negation in which he flounders. But defiance is unfruitful; it saps all inner strength.

This negation begins and ends with the creature world, with those experiences *sans suite* which teach nothing. No matter how vast his experience of life, it never goes deep enough for him to give it meaning. The rudder is gone, and the anchor too. He is condemned to drift. And so the vessel which goes aground on every shoal and reef, which submits helplessly to the buffetings of every storm, must go to pieces finally, become mere flotsam and jetsam. He who would sail the sea of life must become a navigator; he must learn to reckon with wind and tide, with laws and limits. A Columbus does not flout the laws, he extends them. Nor does he set sail for an imaginary world. He discovers a new world accidentally. But such accidents are the legitimate fruits of daring. This daring is not recklessness but the product of inner certitude.

The world which Rimbaud sought as a youth was an impossible world. He made it full, rich, vibrant, mysterious—to compensate for the lack of these qualities in the world he was born into. The impossible world is a world which even the gods never inhabited; it is the Land of Nod which the infant seeks when it has been denied the breast. (It is here the zebus dream probably, and all those other strange animals which dot the shores of the Dead Sea.) Awake, the impossible can only be gained by assault, and the name for this is madness. It may be, as some aver, that it was at the barricades, during the bloody Commune, that Rimbaud swerved from this fatal course. All we know is that suddenly, at the edge of the precipice, he shies away. Definitely *not that!* He behaves as one who has seen through the lies and the delusions. He is not going to be a dupe, a cat's paw. The revolution is as empty and revolting as the everyday life of conformance and submission. Society is nothing but an aggregation of hopeless dolts, scoundrels and fiends. Henceforth he will have faith in nothing but himself. If necessary, he will eat his own dirt. Soon now begins the flight, the aimless wandering, the rudderless drift. All those sordid, despicable realities which he would have none of now become his everyday fare. It is the beginning of the descent, and no thread to guide him out of the dark labyrinth.

The only salvation he recognizes is liberty. And liberty for him is death, as he will discover.

No one has better illustrated the truth than Rimbaud, that the freedom of the isolated individual is a mirage. Only the emancipated individual knows freedom. This freedom is *earned*. It is a gradual liberation, a slow and laborious fight in which the chimeras are exorcised. The chimeras are never slain, for phantoms are only as real as the fears which call them forth. To know oneself, as Rimbaud once counselled in that famous *Letter of the Seer,* is to rid oneself of the demons which possess one. The Church did not invent these terrors of the mind and soul, nor does society create the restrictions which irk and plague one. One church is overthrown and another is set up; one form of society is abolished and another springs up. The powers and emanations persist. Rebels create only new forms of tyranny. Whatever man suffers as an individual all men suffer as members of society. (Abelard came to see that even in the death of a rabbit God also suffers.)

"Everything we are taught is false," Rimbaud protested in his youth. He was right, utterly right. But it is our mission on earth to combat false teaching by manifesting the truth which is in us. Even singlehanded we can accomplish miracles. But the great miracle is to unite all men in the way of understanding. The key *is* Charity. The lies, the falsities, the deceptions, cruel as they are, must be lived through and overcome through integration. The process goes by the hard name of sacrifice.

When Rimbaud denied the inner reality for the outer he put himself in the hands of the dark powers which rule the earth. By refusing to transcend the conditions he was born into he surrendered himself to the stagnant flux. For him the clock did really stop. From then on "he killed time," as we say with unthinking accuracy. No matter how active, the barometer can only register boredom. His activity merely emphasizes his unrelatedness. He is part of the void which he once tried to span with the unsubstantial rainbow of perfection. The Jacob's Ladder of his dreams, once peopled with heralds and messengers from the other world, dissolves. The phantoms take on substance. They become altogether too real, in fact. They are now no longer figments of the imagination but materialized forces of hallucinating reality. He has invoked the aid of powers which refuse to be relegated to the misty deep from which they sprang. Everything is borrowed, everything is vicarious. He is no longer an actor but an agent, or a reagent. In the world of the imagination he had boundless freedom; in the creature world he has empty power, empty possessions. Now he sits neither in the Councils of the Lord nor in the Councils of the Lords: he is in the web of the Powers and Principalities. There is no peace, no surcease from toil. Loneliness and enslavement are his lot. Does an army need rifles? He will supply them—at a profit. It doesn't matter which army, whose army—he will sell to any one who wishes to kill. Kill and be killed, it's all one to him. Is there a market in slaves? He has dealt in coffee, spices, gums, ostrich feathers, muskets . . . why not slaves too? *He* never ordered men to kill one another, nor did he command them to be slaves. But since it *is* so, he will make the most of it. With a nice, clean profit he may possibly retire one day and marry an orphan.

There is nothing too unclean, too unsavory, for him to traffick in. What does it matter? It is no longer *his* world. No, definitely not. It is the world he walked out on—only to enter by the back door. How familiar everything looks now! And that odor of *pourriture*, why, it's positively nostalgic! Even that peculiar smell of burnt horse flesh—or is it his own hide?—is familiar to his nostrils. Thus, as in a mirror darkly, the phantom denizens of his once profound disgust parade before his eyes. He has never injured a soul. No, not he. He even tried to do a little good when he could. Perfectly so. All his life he got nothing but the dirty end of the stick . . . is he to be censured now if he tries to get something for himself, a little of the gravy which is running over but which is always out of reach? So he soliloquizes in the depths of Abyssinia. It is the human giraffe talking to himself in the tall grass of the open veldt. Well may he ask now: *"Qu'est mon néant, auprès de la stupeur qui vous attend?"* What made him superior is that he had no heart. Is it surprising that a man *"sans coeur,"* as he used to sign himself, can spend eighteen years of his life eating his heart out? Baudelaire merely laid his heart bare; Rimbaud plucks his out and devours it slowly.

And so the world gradually comes to resemble the time of the curse. The birds drop from the air, dead before they arrive. The wild beasts gallop to the sea and plunge. The grass withers, the seed rots. Nature takes on the barren, deformed look of a miser, and the heavens mirror the emptiness of the earth. The poet, jaundiced from riding the wild mare over lakes of steaming asphalt, slits its throat. In vain he flaps his rudimentary wings. The fabulous opera collapses and a howling wind rends the props. Save for the furious and most ancient witches, the heath is deserted. Like harpies, armed each and every one with grappling hooks, they fall upon him. Theirs is a more earnest greeting than that visionary brush with his Satanic Majesty. Nothing lacks now to complete the concert of hells he once begged for.

Est-ce la vie encore? Qui sait? On est là enfin, c'est tout ce qu'on peut dire. On va où l'on pèse. Oui. On y va, on y arrive. Et le bateau coule à pic. . . .

In attempting to conquer his demon (the angel in disguise), Rimbaud lived a life such as his worst enemy might have decreed as penalty for attempted evasion from the ranks. It was both the shadow and the substance of his imaginary life, which was rooted in innocence. It was the virgin quality of his soul which made him unadaptable and which, characteristically, led him to a new form of madness—the desire for *total* adaptation, *total* conformity. It is the same old absolutism erupting through the shell of negation. The angel-demon duality, which he finds impossible to resolve, becomes fixed. The only solution is dissolution through number. Unable to be himself, he can become an infinitude of personalities. Jacob Boehme expressed it long ago when he said: "Who dies not before he dies is ruined when he dies." This is the fate which confronts the modern man: rooted in the flux, he does not die but crumbles like a statue, dissolves, passes away into nothingness.

But there is another aspect to Rimbaud's exaggerated worldliness. His desire to possess the truth *in body and soul* is the longing for that nether Paradise which Blake called Beulah. It represents the state of grace of the fully conscious man who, by accepting his Hell unconditionally, discovers a Paradise of his own creation.

This is resurrection *in the flesh*. It means that man at last becomes responsible for his fate. Rimbaud tried to re-situate man on the earth, *this earth,* and completely. He refused to recognize an eternity of the spirit created out of dead bodies. Similarly, he refused to recognize an ideal society composed of soul-less bodies manipulated from their political or economic centers. That terrifying energy which he manifested throughout his career was the creative spirit working through him. If he denies Father and Son he does not deny the Holy Ghost. It is creation he worships, creation he exalts. Out of this fever comes the "need for destruction" sometimes alluded to. It is not a wanton, vengeful destruction that Rimbaud urged, but a clearing of the ground so that fresh shoots may spring up. His whole aim is to give the spirit free rein. Again, by refusing to name, define or delimit the true God, he was endeavoring to create what might be called a plenary vacuum in which the imagination of God could take root. He has not the vulgarity or familiarity of the priest who knows God and talks to Him every day. Rimbaud knew that there was a higher communion of spirit with spirit. He knew that communion is an ineffable duologue which takes place in utter silence, reverence and humility. He is in this respect much nearer to adoration than to blasphemy. His was the enlightenment of those who demand that salvation make sense. The "rational song of the angels"—is it not the persuasion to immediate effort? Postponement is the devil's tune, and with it is always administered the drug of effortlessness.

"How boring! What am I doing here?" writes Rimbaud in one of his letters from Abyssinia. *"What am I doing here?"* That cry of despair epitomizes the plight of the earth-bound. Speaking of the long years of exile which Rimbaud had prophesied for himself in the *Season*, Edgell Rickword remarks: "What he sought when he broke out from his human shell was the means with which to sustain himself in the condition of transcendent purity, of godlike disillusionment in which he emerged." But one never breaks out of this human shell, even in madness. Rimbaud was more like a volcano which, having spent its fires, becomes extinct. If he did emerge at all it was to cut himself off at the height of adolescence. There he remains, poised on the peak, a sort of *jeune roi soleil*.

This refusal to mature, as we view it, has a quality of pathetic grandeur. Mature into *what*? we can imagine him asking himself. Into a manhood which spells enslavement and emasculation?

He had blossomed prodigiously, but—*to flower?* To flower meant to expire in corruption. He elects to die in the bud. It is the supreme gesture of youth triumphant. He will permit his dreams to be massacred, but not to be sullied. He had had a glimpse of life in its splendor and fullness; he would not betray the vision by becoming a domesticated citizen of the world. *"Cette âme égarée parmi nous tous"*—that is how he described himself more than once.

Alone and bereft, he carried his youth to the uttermost limits. He not only commands this realm as it had never before been commanded, but he exhausts it—all that we know of it, at least. The wings with which he soared rot with him in the tomb of the chrysalis from which he refused to emerge. He dies in the womb of his own creation, intact, but in limbo. This quality of the unnatural is his special contribution to the saga of renunciatory acts. It has a monstrous flavor, as "the part of fortune" always has when usurped by the demon. The element of arrest (Narcissism), which is another aspect of the picture, introduces a fear greater than all others —the loss of identity. This threat, which was ever with him, condemned his soul to that oblivion it once despaired of ever attaining. The dream world enfolds him, smothers him, stifles him: he becomes the mummy embalmed by his own artifices.

I like to think of him as the Columbus of Youth, as the one who extended the boundaries of that only partially explored domain. Youth ends where manhood begins, it is said. A phrase without meaning, since from the beginning of history man has never enjoyed the full measure of youth nor known the limitless possibilities of adulthood. How can one know the splendor and fullness of youth if one's energies are consumed in combating the errors and falsities of parents and ancestors? Is youth to waste its strength unlocking the grip of death? Is youth's only mission on earth to rebel, to destroy, to assassinate? Is youth only to be offered up for sacrifice? What of the *dreams* of youth? Are they always to be regarded as follies? Are they to be populated only with chimeras? Dreams are the shoots and buds of the imagination: they have the right to lead pure lives also. Stifle or deform youth's dreams and you destroy the creator. Where there has been no real youth there can be no real manhood. If society has come to resemble a collection of deformities, is it not the work of our educators and preceptors? Today, as yesterday, the youth who would live his own life has no place to turn, no place to live his youth unless, retiring into his chrysalis, he closes all apertures and buries himself alive. The conception of our mother the earth being "an egg which doth contain all good things in it" has undergone a profound change. The cosmic egg contains an addled yolk. That is the present view of mother earth. The psychoanalysts have traced the poison back to the womb, but to what avail? In the light of this profound discovery we are given permission, as I see it, to step from one rotten egg into another. If we believe this it is true, but whether we believe it or not it is pure, unmitigated hell. It is said of Rimbaud that "he scorned the highest satisfactions of our world." Are we not to admire him for that? Why swell the ranks of death and decay? Why breed new monsters of negation and futility? Let society scotch its own rotten corpse! Let us have a new heaven and a new earth!—that was the sense of Rimbaud's obstinate revolt.

Like Columbus, Rimbaud set forth in search of a new route to the Promised Land. The Promised Land of Youth! In his own miserable youth he had fed on the Bible and on the Robinson Crusoe sort of books which children are given to read. One of these, one he was particularly fond of, was called *L'Habitation du Désert*. Singular coincidence, that even as a child he is dwelling in that wilderness which is to be the substance of his life. Did he then, even in that remote time, see himself apart and alone, stranded on a reef, decivilizing himself?

If any man saw with the right and the left eye it was Rimbaud. I speak naturally of the eyes of the soul. With the one he had the power of seeing into eternity; with the other he had the power of seeing into "time and the creatures," as it is written in *The Little Book of the Perfect Life*.

"But these two eyes of the soul of man cannot both perform their work at once," it is said. "If the soul shall see with the right eye into eternity, then the left eye must close itself and refrain from working, and be as though it were dead."

Did Rimbaud close the wrong eye? How else are we to account for his amnesia? That other self which he put on like a suit of armor in order to do battle with the world, did it make him invulnerable? Even armored like a crab, he is as unfit for Hell as he was for Paradise. In no condition, no realm, was it possible for him to remain anchored; he can get a toehold but never a foothold. As though pursued by the Furies, he is driven relentlessly from one extreme to the other.

In some respects he was as un-French as it is possible to be. But in nothing was he more un-

French than in his youthfulness. In him the *gauche,* callow traits which the French loathe were combined to an extraordinary degree. He was as incongruous as a Viking would have been in the court of Louis XIV. "To create a new nature and a correspondingly new art" were, as has been said, his two ambitions. For the France of his day such ideas were as valid and tenable as the worship of a Polynesian idol. Rimbaud has explained, in the letters from Africa, how impossible it was for him to resume the life of a European; he confessed that even the language of Europe had become alien to him. In thought and being he was closer to Easter Island than to Paris, London or Rome. The savage nature which he had manifested from childhood developed more and more with the years; it revealed itself more in his compromises and concessions than in his revolt. He remains the outsider always, playing a lone hand, scornful of the ways and methods he is obliged to adopt. He shows more desire to trample on the world than to conquer over it.

While the zebus dreamed he dreamt too, be sure of it. Only we do not know those dreams of his. We hear only of his complaints and demands, not of his hopes and prayers; we know his scorn and bitterness, but not his tenderness, his longing. We see him preoccupied with a multitude of practical details and we assume that he had killed the dreamer. Yes, it is possible that he stifled his dreams—since they were too grandiose. It is also possible that he played at being sane with the cunning of a super-madman—rather than expire at those radiant horizons which he had opened up. What do we know actually of his interior life in the latter years? Nothing, practically. He had closed up. When he rouses himself it is only to emit a growl, a whine, a curse.

To the anabasis of youth he opposed the katabasis of senility. There was no in-between realm —except the false maturity of the civilized man. The in-between was also the realm of limitations —*cowardly* limitations. No wonder that he saw the saints as strong men, the hermits as artists. They had the strength to live apart from the world, defiant of all but God. They were not worms who bowed and groveled, who said yes to every lie for fear of losing their peace or security. Nor did they fear to lead a totally new life! However, to live apart from the world was not Rimbaud's desire. He loved the world as few men have. Wherever he went his imagination preceded him, opening up glorious vistas which of course always turned out to be mirages. He was concerned only with the unknown. To him the earth was not a dead place reserved for penitent, sorrowful souls who have given up the ghost, but a live, throbbing, mysterious planet where men, if they but realize it, may dwell as kings. Christianity had made of it an eye-sore. And the march of progress was a dead march. About face, then! Resume where the Orient in its splendor left off! Face the sun, salute the living, honor the miracle! He saw that science had become as great a hoax as religion, that nationalism was a farce, patriotism a fraud, education a form of leprosy, and that morals were for cannibals. With every piercing shaft he hit the bull's eye. No one had keener vision, truer aim, than the golden-haired boy of seventeen with the periwinkle blue eyes. *A bas les vieillards! Tout est pourri ici.* He fires point-blank right and left. But he has no sooner laid them low than they stare him in the face again. It is no use shooting at clay pigeons, he thinks to himself. No, the task of demolition demands deadlier weapons. But where is he to get them? At what arsenal?

It is here that the Devil must have stepped in. One can imagine the words he chose . . . "Keep on this way and you'll land in the bug-house. Do you suppose you can kill the dead? Leave that to me, the dead are my meat. Besides, you haven't even begun to live. With your talents the world is yours for the asking. What makes you superior is that you have no heart. Why linger among these rotting, walking cadavers?" To which Rimbaud must have said: *"D'accord!"* Proud, too, that he had wasted no words, man of reason that he was. But, unlike Faust who had inspired him, he forgot to ask the price. Or perhaps he was so impatient that he did not wait to hear the terms of the bargain. It is even possible that he was so naive that he did not suspect there *was* a bargain. For he was always innocent, even as a lost one. It is his innocence which leads him to believe that there is a Promised Land where youth reigns. He believes it even though his hair turns gray. Even when he leaves the farm at Roche for the last time it is not with the idea of dying on a hospital bed in Marseilles but to set sail again for foreign lands. Always his face is turned toward the sun. *Soleil et chair. Et à l'aube c'est le coq d'or qui chante.* In the distance, like an ever-receding mirage, *les villes splendides.* And in the sky the peoples of the earth marching, marching. Everywhere fabulous operas, his own and other men's: creation yielding to creation, paean succeeding paean, infinitude swal-

157

lowing infinitude. *Ce n'est pas le rêve d'un hach-âche, c'est le rêve d'un voyant.*

His was the most terrible deception I know of. He asked for more than any man dared and he received infinitely less than he deserved. Corroded by his own bitterness and despair, his dreams turned to rust. But for us they remain as pure and untarnished as the day they were born. Of the corruption he passed through not a single ulcer adheres. All is white, glistening, tremulous and dynamic, purified by the flames. More than any poet he lodges himself in that vulnerable place called the heart. In all that is broken—a thought, a gesture, a deed, a life—we find the proud Prince of the Ardennes. May his soul rest in peace!

CODA

Rimbaud was born in the middle of the nineteenth century, October 20th, 1854, at 6:00
A.M., it is said. A century of unrest, of material-
ism, and of "progress," as we say. Purgatorial in
every sense of the word, and the writers who
flourished in this period reflect this ominously.
Wars and revolutions were abundant. Russia
alone, we are told, waged thirty-three wars
(mostly of conquest) during the 18th and 19th
centuries. Shortly after Rimbaud is born his
father is off to the Crimean War. So is Tolstoy.
The revolution of 1848, of brief duration but full
of consequences, is followed by the bloody Commune of 1871, which Rimbaud as a boy is
thought to have participated in. In 1848 we in
America are fighting the Mexicans with whom we

are now great friends, though the Mexicans are not too sure of it. During this war Thoreau makes his famous speech on Civil Disobedience, a document which will one day be added to the Emancipation Proclamation—as a rider. Twelve years later the Civil War breaks out, perhaps the bloodiest of all civil wars—but see what we gained! From 1847 until his death in 1881, Amiel is writing his *Journal Intime,* which is the logbook of the sick man of Europe erroneously called Turkey. It gives a thoroughgoing analysis of the moral dilemma in which the creative spirits of the time found themselves. The very titles of the books written by the influential writers of the 19th Century are revelatory. I give just a few . . . *The Sickness Unto Death* (Kierkegaard), *Dreams and Life* (Gérard de Nerval), *Les Fleurs du Mal* (Baudelaire), *Les Chants de Maldoror* (Lautréamont), *The Birth of Tragedy* (Nietzsche), *La Bête Humaine* (Zola), *Hunger* (Knut Hamsun), *Les Lauriers Sont Coupés* (Dujardin), *The Conquest of Bread* (Kropotkin), *Looking Backward* (Edward Bellamy), *Alice in Wonderland* (Lewis Carroll), *The Serpent in Paradise* (Sacher-Masoch), *Les Paradis Artificiels* (Baudelaire), *Dead Souls* (Gogol), *The House of the Dead* (Dostoievsky), *The Wild Duck* (Isben), *The In-*

ferno (Strindberg), *The Nether World* (Gissing), *A Rebours* (Huysmans) . . .

Goethe's *Faust* was not so very old when Rimbaud asked a friend for a copy of it. Remember, the date of his birth is October 20th, 1854. (6:00 A.M. Western Standard Diabolical Time.) The very next year, 1855, *Leaves of Grass* makes its first appearance, followed by general condemnation. In 1860 Baudelaire's work on *les stupéfiants* appears, also followed by condemnation and suppression. Meanwhile *Moby Dick* had come out (1851) and Thoreau's *Walden* (1854). In 1855 Gérard de Nerval commits suicide, having lasted till the remarkable age of 47. In 1854 Kierkegaard is already penning his last words to history, in which he gives us the parable of "The Sacrificed Ones." Just four or five years before Rimbaud completes *A Season in Hell* (1873), Lautréamont publishes privately his celebrated piece of blasphemy, another "work of youth," as we say, in order not to take these heartbreaking testaments seriously. (How many authors in this 19th Century publish their first works privately!) By 1888 Nietzsche is explaining to Brandes that he can now boast of three readers: Brandes, Taine and Strindberg. The next year he goes mad and remains that way until his death in 1900. Lucky man! From 1893 to 1897 Strindberg is experiencing a *crise*, as the French put it, which he describes with magistral effects in the *Inferno*. Reminiscent of Rimbaud is the title of another of his works: *The Keys to Paradise*. In 1888 comes Dujardin's curious little book, forgotten until recently. In the same year Edward Bellamy's Utopian document is published. By this time Mark Twain is at his height, *Huckleberry Finn* having appeared in 1884, the same year as *Against the Grain* of Huysmans. By the fall of 1891, the year of Rimbaud's death, Knut Hamsun is directing discussions in which "the right of the obscure and the mysterious in literature" is being fought over. In that same year Gissing's *New Grub Street* is launched. It is an interesting year in 19th Century literature, this year of Rimbaud's death; it ends a decade in which a number of writers important to the 20th Century are born. Here are a few titles of books which appeared in the year of 1891, curious books in that they differ so widely one from another ... *Gösta Berling, The Light that Failed, The Little Minister, The Picture of Dorian Grey, Les Cahiers d'André Walter, Le Livre de la Pitié et de la Mort, Adventures of Sherlock Holmes, Là-Bas, The Fruits of Civilization, The End of Sodom, Tess of the D'Urbervilles, Sixtine (roman de la vie cérébrale)* ...

What a century of names! Let me include a few I have not mentioned . . . Shelley, Blake, Stendhal, Hegel, Fechner, Emerson, Poe, Schopenhauer, Max Stirner, Mallarmé, Tchekov, Andreyev, Verlaine, Couperus, Maeterlinck, Madame Blavatsky, Samuel Butler, Claudel, Unamuno, Conrad, Bakunin, Shaw, Rilke, Stefan George, Mary Baker Eddy, Verhaeren, Gautier, Léon Bloy, Balzac, Yeats . . .

What revolt, what disillusionment, what longing! Nothing but crises, breakdowns, hallucinations and visions. The foundations of politics, morals, economics and art tremble. The air is full of warnings and prophecies of the débâcle to come—and in the 20th Century it comes! Already two world wars and a promise of more before the century is out. Have we touched bottom? Not yet. The moral crisis of the 19th Century has merely given way to the spiritual bankruptcy of the 20th. It is "the time of the assassins," and no mistaking it. Politics has become the business of gangsters. The peoples are marching in the sky but they are not shouting hosannahs; those below are marching towards the bread lines. *C'est—l'aube exaltée ainsi qu'un peuple de colombes . . .*

163